SPARK

SPARK

CREATING YOUR UNIQUE
PATHWAY TO SUCCESS,
HAPPINESS, AND FULFILLMENT

Serge Karim Ganem

COPYRIGHT © 2017 SERGE KARIM GANEM
All rights reserved.

SPARK

Creating Your Unique Pathway to Success, Happiness, and Fulfillment

ISBN 978-1-61961-787-2 *Paperback*
       978-1-61961-788-9 *Ebook*
       978-1-61961-789-6 *Audiobook*

To Noemie, my wife and beloved muse, and my children, Elia and Zacharie. I also dedicate this book to the child that lives inside each one of us.

CONTENTS

FOREWORD 9

PREFACE 11

INTRODUCTION 13

1. UNEARTHING WHO YOU REALLY ARE 21
2. THE IMPORTANCE OF DREAMS 45
3. THE ADVERSITY GAME 59
4. GIVING YOURSELF PERMISSION 83
5. BECOMING A CREATOR 91
6. THE BIGGER PICTURE 109
7. LOVE ALWAYS WINS 121
8. THE END OF COMPETITION 135

CONCLUSION 147

ACKNOWLEDGEMENTS 155

ABOUT THE AUTHOR 157

FOREWORD

Initially, I was excited to work on this project with Karim because I viewed it as a book about creativity, which is always one of my favorite topics. Then, a little more than a week into our time working together, I found out I was pregnant. The timing turned out to be incredibly fortuitous.

As my pregnancy wore on and my worldview evolved as a result, I became more and more intrigued by some of the other ideas contained in this book. What I began seeing through Karim's thoughts and words was a vision of how I want to raise my daughter. At the core, it turns out *Spark* encapsulates my biggest dreams for her—that she embrace and bring into the world the truest version of herself; that she build a life that looks not how it's supposed to look but how she wants it to look; that she be a creator, whatever that may mean for her; and that she live in a world where she is surrounded by love and a supportive, cocreating community.

As I look back on the experience, it strikes me that it was no accident that Karim and *Spark* appeared in my life when they did. There's an auspiciousness and synchronicity to it all, which is fitting because, in many ways, those same elements are embedded in the heart of this book.

—NIKKI VAN NOY FAULLS, EDITOR

PREFACE

Imagine this. You are living a life in which everything you do—whether in your personal, professional, or private emotional life—corresponds exactly with the person you are. All of your thoughts, actions, and energy are united. They work cohesively to move you in the specific, chosen direction that resonates deeply with you. There's no doubt that this direction is the right one because all of your decisions are aligned with who you truly are.

Imagine that at this very moment you can be, experience, and feel every single nuance of who you are. Not who you're told you should be or believe you should be, but who you actually are. Can you see how everything becomes not only possible but also incredibly achievable?

This is how we embrace our individual pathway to greatness. This is how we experience the spark.

INTRODUCTION

IGNITING YOUR SPARK

We all have a spark within us just waiting to be set ablaze. If yours hasn't been ignited yet, it's only a matter of time. Or maybe your spark has already been lit, but you're not quite aware of it yet. I know that's how it worked for me. One of the great ironies of life is that, so often, we are unaware of the significance of an event or moment until long after it has passed. It's only later, down the road, that life places that turn of events into its proper context.

One morning in 2006, I was sitting on a bench outside a café in the Upper West Side of Manhattan. A few days before, my father had passed away. Despite the fact that I knew he was sick and the possibility of his recovery was slim, I was nonetheless in a state of shock. I didn't feel destroyed, like I had expected; instead, I felt an odd surge of energy unlike anything I'd ever experienced before. I was only twenty-seven at the time—little more than a child, really. I was still in the process of becoming a fully formed version of myself. Little did I know then that this particular moment would serve as a huge stepping-stone in getting me to that point. In retrospect, I'd say there was a whole lot of energy inside of me swirling around, doing its work to make me not just a better person, but a more whole and authentic person.

As I sat on the bench that morning, I was so aware and alive that, when I look back, it feels as though that singular instant either never happened at all or somehow went on forever. I became aware of the beautiful morning light filtering through the leaves that hung above me and of the fact that I was in New York City, the city of my dreams. I felt a sense of amazement about my own life, as memories of all the things I had done to become a part of this city flooded my mind.

I also realized that I was not completely fulfilled.

A rush of insights came next, presenting themselves as feelings rather than thoughts. They felt alive and pulsating. I thought about my father and how he was still so young when he died. I wondered if I would die young, too. "If I am going to live a short life," I thought, "I need to live a very good life before my time is up." I pondered what constituted a good life and whether I was actually living one. I considered how I spent most of my days, and wondered what I could start doing now to ensure I didn't have any regrets. Sometimes my work excited me, but corporate branding wasn't really what I wanted to do: It didn't feel like a calling. I was successful enough, but I wasn't fulfilled.

Then, suddenly, it all became very clear. I understood that some things in my life aligned with my essence—that core and totally unique part of us that remains consistent from birth through death—while others did not. It struck me that those things that fell into the latter category were unnecessary. They weren't bad—because nothing in life is either completely good or bad—but they didn't align with who I was or where I wanted to go. But where did I want to go? In that moment of consciousness and clarity, I realized that I needed to steer my life in the direction that aligned with my essence.

I sat there lost in my thoughts. I can't be sure if seconds passed or hours, but suddenly, I noticed that a well-dressed man clad entirely in white was also sitting on the bench.

"What's up, son?" the old man asked, turning toward me.

The way he looked at me, it seemed almost as if he somehow knew I'd experienced a loss.

As I tuned back in to the world around me, I became aware of the fact that the old man was finding something positive to say to each person who walked by. Little things like, "I like your dog," or "Nice outfit!" Everyone he spoke to smiled or replied kindly in response. Clearly, these passersby were used to the man's presence and thoughtful words. It struck me what a commitment it was to dole out so much good energy to every single person who walked by. It was like this man was giving each person a little gift.

I used to get coffee from the very same café we were sitting in front of every single morning on my way to work. How had I never noticed this colorful man before? If I didn't know any better, I would think I had conjured him up.

As we settled back into a comfortable silence, I considered the trickle-down effect he was having on all the people passing by. They might go into their offices feeling a little bit better because of this man and say something nice to a coworker. Their words could, in turn, have a similar effect on the coworker, who would go on to say something nice to a client, and so on and so forth, creating a beautiful chain reaction of kindness. In fact, this one man may very well have made a much bigger impact on the world than even he imagined.

"What am I doing to make the world better?" I wondered. What was I doing to bring my essence up to the surface? Not enough, I realized. Just like that, it struck me that I should probably quit my job. I should follow a path that would allow me to make the most of my essence, just like this man next to me was doing…and my father had not. Looking back, I now understand that it was at this precise instant—just as my father's spark flickered out—that my own was lit.

By the time I walked away from that bench, I was determined to follow a path completely different from the one I had been following up to that point. A few days later, I quit my job. My girlfriend—now my wife—Noemie did the same, and we spent the next four months traveling and discovering not only the world but ourselves. It was the beginning of me learning how to follow my own path—the path that best expresses my essence and allows me to bring my unique gifts into the world.

In this way, I've ensured that whenever my time comes, I will be able to rest peacefully in the fact that I lived a good life—a life that was a full expression of myself and that allowed me to share my unique genius with the world.

When we embrace who we truly are at our core and trust where it leads us, there is no way we can do anything but lead a successful life.

Most books about achieving success involve checklists of sorts. There are certain requirements we need to fulfill to get from point A to point B. The type of success we're talking about here is just the opposite. There are no formulas. There is certainly no checklist. There is no preset path. For each one of us, achieving this sort of success is a unique process. We must each not just follow but blaze our own path to get there. What this book will do is help you discover that pathway for yourself. As you make your way down that path, you will find that your spark gets brighter and brighter, until it completely illuminates the road in front of you.

My own pathway opened up to me that day on the bench. By witnessing how important and meaningful the small actions of that man were to the people around him, I suddenly understood that everything we do—no matter how insignificant it may seem—is extremely important. When we are aware of what we have to offer the world, we stop merely observing life, and our potential becomes endless. This includes the potential for our own lives and the potential we have to positively impact others and the world.

WHAT I'VE LEARNED SINCE FINDING MY SPARK

I've been lucky enough and worked hard enough to achieve my fair share of success in this life. I have been an entrepreneur for nearly two decades. In this time, I have launched many successful technology projects and several companies, including some very disruptive ones in Europe.

Despite my material accomplishments, I can honestly say that I consider the most beautiful enterprise, ambitious project, and greatest reward any of us can give ourselves to be a good life. A good life can mean a lot of different things, but I'm talking about the kind of life where your actions are aligned with your essence. The kind of life that is a reflection of who you are on the deepest and truest level. When we achieve this, there are no more limits.

My goal is to help you identify your spark, just as I did on an Upper West Side bench years ago. Once you do this, limitlessness will follow, and friction and fear will fall away.

Of course, this isn't to say that the process of getting to this point is easy. Recognizing and embracing our unique gifts and then following them where they lead us requires courage. It is an act of bravery to be able to look at ourselves in the mirror and say, "I don't know where this genius of mine is going to take me, but I know it's important, because it's uniquely mine. And I'm going to follow it wherever it leads me."

The beginning, my friends, is the most important part of the journey. As we move forward together, always remember that the point here is never to change yourself, nor to be different from how or who you are today. The point is to find yourself and to bring the expression of yourself into the world. Once you've realized that you, like everyone else in our world, are a unique person with unique gifts to share, and a unique path to walk, the possibilities are endless. Not only will you light your own life on fire, but you will also step up to light the world on fire.

And it all starts with a little spark...

CHAPTER ONE

UNEARTHING WHO YOU REALLY ARE

"Nothing is more powerful than an idea whose time has come."

—VICTOR HUGO

Have you ever experienced this feeling? You are in a car that is rapidly moving toward a destination only you know. As you look out the driver's side window, you see trees appearing and disappearing so quickly that they seem to be moving by themselves. In front of you, the road looks as though it's unfolding itself smoothly from the horizon. Inside, the car is quiet, and you are comfortable and peaceful.

Part of this contentment you feel comes from the knowledge that you are headed down the right road. If circumstances don't change, you'll soon be at your destination, which makes your journey even more enjoyable.

Suppose now that the road is your life and this feeling of heading in the right direction can be experienced because you are utterly sure of exactly where you are going. You don't have to know all of the twists and turns in the road ahead because you already know the most important thing—that you're moving in the right direction.

Of course, this sense of assurance in who we are and where we're going can be easier said than done because we all experience self-doubt. Rest assured, uniqueness—which is just another word for "essence"—is a universal gift that is bestowed upon each and every one of us. Yes, that includes you! Like fingerprints, no two people's essences are alike. The more we get in touch with who we are, and the more we let labels drop away, the easier it will be to see those special traits and characteristics that live within us, and within us alone. The more we can see these qualities and gifts within ourselves, the easier and more natural it is to bring them into the world and allow them to guide us.

Uniqueness is the potential that lies within us. Once the spark is lit, that uniqueness is activated, and we can begin to bring potential into reality by expressing ourselves fully and completely through how we interact, how unabashedly we allow our true essence to be seen by the world, and what we create. The expression of our individual essence allows us to express and manifest our lives in the unique way appropriate only for us.

When we connect with our unique essence, we also connect with our most profound desires, and we accept and love ourselves wholly and completely. We are also able to love and accept the people around us more wholly and completely for who they are. For when we recognize that we are unique, we also inherently understand how unique and special every other person is. We tap into not only our potential, but the entire world's potential.

DISCOVERING YOUR OWN GENIUS

Perhaps you're a bit skeptical about all of this. Maybe you don't feel very unique or special at all. I get it. Through our education, work, and social environments, we have been conditioned to believe that geniuses are one in a million, that most people are not creative, that if you want to have an impact on the world, you need to suffer, and that we don't really have much choice in it all. These are just ideas, and ideas are not facts. So, for just a moment, consider a new way of looking at things.

You are a genius. If you don't believe that, it's just because you haven't yet unearthed your own personal brand of genius. Sure, you're probably not a genius at everything, but I guarantee you that you're a genius at something. If you find yourself in a situation that is unsatisfying or in a job where you feel like you're losing power, time, energy, or effort, it's a sign you are not yet aware of where specifically your genius lies. But that doesn't mean it's not there!

It's important to understand that genius takes lots of different shapes. Many of us have bought into society's narrow parameters of what genius looks like, so discovering our own genius may require us to first shed those preconceived notions.

It's okay when society at large doesn't recognize our strengths or genius. What's important is that we learn to recognize, observe, and cultivate our own genius and strengths. Language can get us in trouble here because, sometimes, we do not have a specific word for a type of genius. When we cannot define things, we tend to think they don't exist. This is not true. It likely just means that your brand of genius is unique, which is even more wonderful because it proves that you bring something uniquely you into the world.

When we accept the fact that something can exist without

being defined, we are seizing the opportunity to create something new. Once we recognize and embrace this, other people have the opportunity to do the same thing—to look at the world in a different way and realize, "Oh, I haven't noticed that before, but it's there. It exists."

RECOGNIZING OUR LITTLE CREATOR

One key to uncovering our unique brand of genius is getting in touch with our inner child or, as I like to call it, our little creator. As adults, we all suffer from amnesia. We forget that, no matter how old we are, on some level, our inner child continues to live on. For some of us who might associate our younger years with suffering, negative experiences, or painful emotions, the idea of an eternal inner child is a scary or painful notion. We want to forget about our childhood and be done with it. For others, the responsibilities of the real, adult world are so pressing that it's impossible to connect with the idea of youth and all the freedom that comes with it.

Whatever our past or present situation may be, our inner child should not be discounted. It's important to understand that although our childhood lasts for a finite amount of time, our inner child is infinite and ever-present. We all have one, and he or she is an extremely powerful being. Our inner child can play and create. A child doesn't approach reality from the rigid standpoint of how things are. A child creates new experiences and considers each situation from a fresh vantage point. Our inner child knows it's okay to take an uncharted pathway as opposed to blindly following a prescribed way of doing things. Our inner child can fearlessly and wholeheartedly acknowledge his or her own genius.

We human beings often have a hard time accepting duality, but it nonetheless exists within each of us. We are simultaneously adults and still children. We are weak in some areas and strong in others. The more we accept these seeming dichotomies, the more our inner child will thrive. The more our inner child thrives, the greater our capacity to be creative, to think outside the box, and to connect with others and the world as emotional beings. We can live our lives in a more truthful, authentic way because children never lie. They may shout, laugh, or cry, but whatever the expression is, it's honest. A child will never tell you a situation is great or pretend something is working when it's not.

When we are disconnected from our inner child, it is extremely difficult to connect with who we really are, with our gifts and strengths. They become lost in the shuffle of fears, responsibilities, and rigidity. Tragically, this disconnect means we miss out on the richest part of ourselves, our essence.

When we are connected with our essence, we exist in a state of self-love. We can make decisions from the place that most reflects our deepest desires and allows our own brand of genius to thrive. When we achieve self-love, there aren't many choices left, except to follow the pathway in life that allows for the fullest and most fulfilling expression of who we are. We say yes to ourselves. Our capacity to create, achieve, and share with others is vast. It is, in the truest sense of the word, freedom.

EIGHT NEW WAYS TO LOOK AT THE WORLD AND YOUR PLACE IN IT

Much of what we're talking about goes against what we've been programmed to do, think, and believe. We've been programmed to doubt ourselves, to believe we're nothing special, and to act like adults. Breaking through these patterns can be difficult, but it becomes easier once we start to look at the world through new eyes.

Following are a few ideas to consider that just might tweak how you look at the world and your place in it. These ideas, when translated into action, might just set you free.

#1: IT TOOK HUNDREDS OF THOUSANDS OF YEARS TO GET TO YOU

When we embrace our unique nature, we acknowledge the miracle of our existence. If you're not yet buying how special and unrepeatable you are, I want you to at least consider how big you are. In fact, you are much, much bigger than you've probably even begun to realize. In that singular body of yours, you encapsulate the living story of humankind. It took generation upon generation upon generation over the course of 200,000 years to get to you. You are the final result of all that time and history. You are the manifestation of all of these people, their cells, hopes, and dreams. All of the potential of everyone who came before you now lives inside of you. How could there possibly be anyone like you? How could you be anything but unique?

As we start to come into this awareness of our own unique nature, it's important to remind ourselves of where we come from. Not only do we have potential within us, but we are also the manifestation of so many other people's potential. All these lives, possibilities, and types of uniqueness are alive within and through us. Our cells are not just our cells: they are the combination and culmination of all of those who came before us.

This means that, while the concepts we're talking about

may sound abstract, they're not only factual, but grounded in biology. At the most basic level, we are our cells, and our cells hold memories. Not only our memories, but the memories of all our ancestors, dating back to the beginning of human kind. This is not a spiritual idea but a scientific fact. Procreation begins with one winning cell joining another, and that winner is you. You've already won at life just by beating the odds and being here. You are already a success, even if you were never to achieve anything else from that moment forward.

#2: YOU CREATE YOUR OWN HISTORY

While our origins stretch far back through the annals of humankind, each of us creates our own history based on how we connect with our own lives. We spend so much time talking about how we can create our future, but we don't spend much time talking about how we can also create our own history. Think about this powerful truth: we can create whatever we want, including recreating ourselves at this very moment if we so choose.

First of all, what is history? Factual events may have happened in the past, but that's not the same as history. History is a story, and those stories originate from our memories. Therefore, there is no history if there is no memory, and memory is subjective. You and I may live through precisely the same situation, but we remember it quite differently. Our versions of history are different, but they're still both correct and valid. Each of us is the author of our own history.

Since our memories consist of a combination of thoughts, emotions, beliefs, intentions, relationships, places, and events, when we define our history, what we are essentially doing is defining our lives. The history we create for ourselves is not something static, because we may not feel the same today as we did five years ago, which means our perception shifts. In other words, the present moment defines not only who we are, but who we were. It's also important to remember that anything we do today will become a part of our history—so let's make that history count. Let's embrace every single moment, because it's important both to who we are becoming and who we have been.

#3: YOU ARE THE CENTER OF THE UNIVERSE

If the universe is infinite, that means there is no center. Or perhaps everywhere is the center. It's such an arbitrary concept, really, who's to say you're not the center of the universe?

So far, we've talked about the vastness of entities outside

us, like humanity and time. Sometimes the contemplation of these topics can be enough to make us feel very, very small in the grand scheme of things. But we, as individuals, are also vast. In fact, there is an entire universe inside of us. Take your brain, for example. There are approximately 100 billion neurons in your brain, as many neurons as there are stars in the galaxy. And that's only the beginning! Your neurons are composed of molecules, your molecules of atoms, and your atoms of energy.

You can plunge deeper and deeper within, as though you yourself were deep space. This entire layered universe inside you just keeps running smoothly every day, without your even thinking about it. Imagine how much power that means we have churning inside of us every moment of every day. Imagine how much space there is inside of you that could never be duplicated inside anyone else. Imagine that potential. Rest assured, you are anything but small!

#4: YOUR PERCEPTION DEFINES YOUR WORLD

As you can see, everything boils down to perception—history, time, even who we are. When we think of ourselves and the universe in these terms, we can see how important our vantage point is. Ultimately, everything is relative. As we observe the galaxy around us, it seems almost infinite. However, the galaxy is small in the face of the entire cosmos.

We can apply this same line of reasoning to thoughts and dreams. We may view a little kid's dream as essentially meaningless in the grand scheme of things. With all the ideas and dreams all human beings have in total, why does the one dream of this one child mean anything? That little dream is just a small galaxy in a massive cosmos. However, if we shift our perspective a little bit, we could also argue that inside this child's infinite mind, there is untold potential: an entire world and future could be impacted by the dreams and ideas of this single child. When we look at it this way, this child's dream is precious and huge.

I would argue that if there's one thing we should take seriously in life, it's children's dreams and ideas. They are unfiltered and unclouded by so many of the things that impede us as adults. Children have not yet had the chance to write a history for themselves that impacts their vision, hopes, and creativity. This brings us back to the importance of nurturing our inner child. When we acknowledge our inner child, we can access our pure dreams, filled with potential. There is infinite power in every dream we have as children.

In some ways, we are each our own universe, comingling

with the universes of the people we encounter and interact with. Sometimes we may feel as though we're alone or separated from others, but we're not. We all live as part of a collective. Other people's universes affect ours.

Think back to that child for a minute. If you were to support his dreams and encourage him, you would likely be playing a role in helping him to believe in his potential and to create and dream on an even larger scale. On the other hand, if you brush off his dreams, you are sending the message that his ideas don't matter and he should keep them to himself. Not only that, but when you recognize this child's unique value, it becomes easier for him to see the unique value of others, which starts to create a wonderful trickle-down effect, promoting more potential.

There is a lot of power in this—power that we all need to be aware of. As human beings, we can easily let ourselves be swayed and defined by those around us, despite the fact that they are merely observers of our reality and who we are. Yes, when observation is supportive, it can be helpful and promote growth and the expression of uniqueness. However, it's also important to realize there is only one person who can truly observe the space and time of where you are at the present moment, and that is you.

To believe in yourself and your full potential, to bring your complete essence to everything you do, it's important that you have the confidence to trust yourself above all others. The difference between your observations of yourself and others' observations of you is that your observations are based in your experience. They are real. The observations of others are merely judgments or labels applied to identify who you are based on external standards. This is key: to turn the spark within you into a flame that the world can see, you have to believe that what you see and feel is real, can be trusted, and can be built upon. You have to believe in yourself, no matter what anyone else thinks or says.

This isn't to say that what other people think is bad or wrong if it differs from your perception. It's just another point of view. Have you ever heard the story about the blind men and the elephant? It goes like this: A group of blind men are standing around an elephant, each with his hands placed upon one of the elephant's body parts.

The man touching the elephant's leg says, "Oh, it's long and heavy."

The man with his hand in the elephant's mouth says, "It's very wet!"

The man touching the elephant's tail says, "It's short and thin."

None of the men are wrong; they are just observing the elephant from different perspectives. The things they're explaining are so disparate, though, that if one of these men was not firm in his experience, he might very well start to second-guess what he was feeling, although he was right all along.

#5: YOU ARE UNIQUE, NOT DIFFERENT

While viewpoints may differ from one person to the next, we are not inherently different from one another. Each of us is merely unique. This is an important distinction, because the word "different" suggests that we are dissimilar to something and, therefore, acts as a measurement of sorts. There is an implied comparison, as well as the insinuation that there is a standard to be measured against. It means that we are being defined by others rather than by ourselves.

With the notion of uniqueness comes an acknowledgement of standing on one's own. When we are unique, we are empowered, measured by no one's standards but our own. When it comes to our essence, there is no standard. There is only who we are, and that is inherently perfect just as it is. Where "different" must by nature always be compared to something else, "unique" stands alone.

Another problem with the notion of difference as it pertains to our unique essence is that it lowers our potential. When we identify two things as "different," this is often accompanied by the urge to define one of those things as better or greater than. We see people as they should be rather than how they are. Or we believe that there are only a certain number of different categories that we must fit into, which is limiting. When we stop comparing things, we also stop trying to control them and can allow things to simply exist on their own merit. When we achieve this mind-set, we can stop judging ourselves or buying into the idea that there is a model or standard for how we should be. We can stop believing there's something greater than what we inherently are, or that the things that make us unique are somehow a weakness.

#6: THERE'S NO PLACE LIKE HOME

When you accept your unique self, a peaceful, contented state of mind will set in, like you're meeting an old friend. You will feel more settled and stable than ever before, with no more questions or doubts about who you are or what you should be doing. It is delightfully freeing and empowering. You will find that you no longer feel the need to justify who you are. You won't feel the need to convince anyone else—least of all yourself—that you are worthy or are taking the right action in a given scenario. Your energy will be redirected from all these things, and you can begin to focus on the pathway your unique nature instinctively directs you toward. You will come home to yourself.

This all sounds great, right? So how do we get there? How do we learn who our unique self is and decide to embrace it? It's simple: we just say yes—yes to uniqueness and yes to ourselves. From this point forward, there is no more becoming, because we already are.

When we have accepted ourselves as the unique creatures we are, we can relax and observe as we let our true selves flow. Within that flow, our uniqueness has the space to be and to grow. Our only job is to honor and observe—but not judge!—it. We can honor not only our uniqueness, but also ourselves for allowing the experience of this state of freedom. We can be grateful and joyful because we have come home to ourselves.

In these early stages of acceptance, our unique essence is almost like a baby. It's small, fragile, and probably the most important thing in life. It is a part of us, and it's up to us to foster its growth by continuing to say yes. Also, as is the case with a baby, we don't know what that growth is going to be like or where we will find ourselves next. We now have to make a choice: Are we going to say yes again? Are we going to continue nurturing our uniqueness so that it can lead us down a new pathway that hasn't yet come fully into sight?

Being seen and accepted by the world, and embracing everything that makes us, begins with being seen and accepted by ourselves. This acceptance doesn't have anything to do with perfection. In fact, it's the opposite. It's recognizing that beautiful glittering spark of uniqueness within ourselves for everything that it is, just as it is. This includes weaknesses and imperfections as much as strengths. It's about stoking that spark by observing, accepting, and giving ourselves permission to be us.

As we give ourselves permission to fall deeper and deeper into the natural flow of who we are, we can create things that are bigger than ourselves. It could be anything! Take the old man on the bench: what he was creating wasn't tactile, but its positive impact was nonetheless undeniable and transformative. Creation flows from this new acceptance of ourselves because we can now begin to reconcile our inner child with who we are, today as adults, which results in a powerful combination of dreams and, most importantly, a feeling of responsibility to those dreams. We can reconcile the conscious with the unconscious, and act from there.

#7: YOU DEFINE SUCCESS

While this acceptance of ourselves is some of the most important work we will ever do, both in terms of our own fulfillment and what we can bring into the world, it's not always easy. It certainly requires some big adjustments.

When we embrace our uniqueness, and allow it to flow, we must also release the labels that we're taught to identify with. Of course, that doesn't mean that society will stop labeling us based on our profession, background, ethnicity, or anything else, but it does mean that we detach from these exterior definitions and categorizations. When we stay attached to labels, we allow them to define us. This idea of categorization simply doesn't work in the face of uniqueness; in fact, it defies it.

Of course, it will still be true that we have a certain profession, background, or ethnicity, but detachment means we don't identify with or place unnecessary meaning upon those labels. We realize that we're much more than that. We are unique creatures with unlimited potential. We are our own creators. We are potential incarnate. We are the collection of every single second of our life—every emotion, every encounter, and every experience—leading up to the present. No one can define us, and the very second we truly become aware of that, we also become numb to all definition. We can be anything we want.

One of the biggest labels we put on ourselves in the Western world today is the label of success. Our quest for and fixation on success can be an extremely difficult habit to shed. Nonetheless, if we concentrate on the internal rather than the external, we have to completely redefine success.

Success can no longer equate to status or power; instead, it must be the state of mind in which the love we have for ourselves is free of external conditions. Success must be the ability to trust, love, and embrace ourselves through every single moment of our lives. The irony is that this new definition of success often leads directly to external signs of success. The distinction is that these external signs of success are now the result of following our true path, rather than hunting them down as a means of validating ourselves.

There are two primary problems with the way we look at success today. First, we label someone successful because of what's on her résumé, the amount of money he's making, or the relationship she's in. I would argue that true success is living the type of life in which we avoid labels altogether. When we define success by labels, we completely miss out on the essence of who someone is.

Second, we need to stop looking toward the future and start looking at this very moment. No more saying, "When

I accomplish X, then I will be successful," because that future never arrives. It is only a concept. On no day of your life will the present moment be the future. When we pin our notion of success on a future outcome, it is and will always remain an elusive ideal dangling out there in front of us, making us feel as though we don't have or aren't enough.

The real question we should gauge success by is: Do I feel powerful, amazing, outstanding, and peaceful right now? If we are not feeling these things, we are probably not successful enough, no matter what sort of titles, labels, or accolades we have acquired. To lead truly meaningful lives, success is something we should feel every single day in the course of day-to-day living: "I am successful because I am living a life I love right now."

Once we stop worrying about letting some future success define us, we each get to define the rules of our own lives. With that, we also get to define what we believe about ourselves and our reality. If we happen to be feeling stuck in life right now, we can just change the rules so that's no longer the case! We wrote whatever guidelines are making us feel stuck, which means we can also change them. Even if we're playing by someone else's rules, we still hold the power to define our own rules because, at some point, consciously or subconsciously, we agreed to their standards. All we have to do is change our minds and make up new parameters for ourselves.

#8: STRIVE FOR ABUNDANCE

To understand success in this new context, we also have to understand the difference between richness and abundance. "Richness" refers to the amount of wealth we have acquired. "Abundance" can be defined as the ability to get what we want at the very moment when we need it. Abundance does not require accumulation, but it does require us to be creators and generators, which is very much aligned with what our unique nature does. Mind you, this is not to say that money is bad or that we have to shun it if we are to be the best version of ourselves. Money is neither good nor bad. What matters is what we do with money, and from that perspective, we can think of money as energy.

People who refuse the flow of money energy because they think it's somehow wrong also refuse the good—even great—things that can be done with it. If we really want to be ready for something great—which is precisely where our unique pathway leads us—then we also have to be ready to consider the fact that money is often a key factor in exchanges of all varieties.

This doesn't mean money has to be involved in everything, but it does mean that we have to acknowledge the fact that the economy is a big part of the world we live in. Any project that springs from our uniqueness and wants to be grounded may very well at some point necessitate money. As we look at success in this new paradigm, we must remember: money itself is neutral. It's the things we do with it that are important and meaningful—and flowing and creating in service of our unique and true essence is always meaningful.

CHAPTER TWO

THE IMPORTANCE OF DREAMS

"Reality is merely an illusion, albeit a very persistent one."
—ALBERT EINSTEIN

I was a very shy kid who didn't like to talk much. The less interaction I had with people, the better I felt. It wasn't that I didn't like company so much as the idea having to interact with others made me so uncomfortable that I preferred not to. Adults, in particular, made me really nervous.

Because of this, I spent a lot of time listening to conversations adults didn't think I understood and observing their words and behavior. I learned a lot by doing this, and I came to appreciate and understand feelings, perception, and body language.

My reserved composition and demeanor also left me with a lot of time to daydream, which further shaped my ability to observe. I have brought this into my adult life—I take the time to observe life and let it flow around me. It has shaped my view of the world and my ability to create a vision for my future self. For me, it's in these moments of letting go and just being, letting my brain wander, where the spark occurs and information can be received.

A lot of my childhood reservations (which ended up benefitting me in the long run) may have come from the fact that, although I wasn't always consciously aware of it, I now understand that I've always been perceived as different. For the first several years of my life, I was unaware that people considered me different because, of course, it wasn't something that most people came out and told me. Growing up in France, I was probably one out of one thousand people in the entire nation who had one Jewish parent and one Muslim parent—my mother was Jewish and my father was Muslim.

My parents separated when I was young, which was perhaps why I assumed they were the same religion for so long. This misconception of mine is sort of funny in retrospect, but, as a kid, it made sense. Neither of my parents ate pork for religious reasons, so I naturally assumed it was for the same reason. I certainly noticed there were some instances in which my father did one thing and my mother did another, but I never put too much thought into it.

It wasn't until I raised the idea of a bar mitzvah to my father when I was around ten years old that I first understood my parents subscribed to different faiths. My dad was completely open to the idea of a bar mitzvah but also told me that he could not participate.

"If you would like one, that's okay," he told me, "but I cannot help you. You will have to ask your grandfather."

To this day, I admire how respectful my father was of the situation and how he refrained from pushing me in any direction other than what I chose for myself.

GOING AGAINST THE GRAIN OF CULTURAL NORMS

Over the years, I've come to understand that the confusion my situation caused others goes back to the labels we discussed in the previous chapter. I understood from a very young age that people love when you are just one easily classifiable thing. This was certainly true growing up in Europe in the 1980s; you could not belong to too many circles. People wanted a clear-cut idea of who you were. Based on that definition, there was a set classification of things you should do and be.

During my childhood, France was a very conservative country with a lot of judgment and preconceived ideas about things like religion and integration. At the time, France was largely Catholic. Even the few of us who weren't Catholic understood Catholicism because it was everywhere.

In the grand scope of history, France was still rebuilding after a couple of wars and, because of this, wanted people to be integrated. Being Jewish was a problem. Being Muslim was a problem. Being Jewish *and* Muslim doubled that problem. Once I became aware of who I was and what made me different, I came to understand that it wasn't just my classmates who thought of me as some sort of extraterrestrial—it was their parents as well. Sometimes I felt as though I was speaking a different language than everyone else around me, as if I were a foreigner in my own land.

A DIVIDED SELF

Although I can retrospectively articulate what I felt as a

child, I'm not sure I could have pinpointed my feelings back then. Today I understand that I spent a lot of my formative years feeling uncomfortable and conflicted. It was as if the world around me was telling me I needed to divide up and cordon off the parts of myself that society viewed as being in conflict with one another. This felt unnatural. How could I divvy up and hide parts of myself? I wanted to embrace both my Jewish and Muslim lineage.

In recent years, I have spoken with others from mixed ethnic and multicultural backgrounds, and it seems my experience as a child wasn't unusual. Like me, they began their lives completely unaware that anything about their situation could be perceived as abnormal. And then, for each of them, there was a specific moment when, all of a sudden, they realized others didn't view them as normal.

In some ways, I think most of us experience some version of this during childhood. We are largely blissfully unaware of our circumstances until someone else points out the ways in which our life doesn't fit into a box. This human tendency to focus on differences has always confused me. It's like distinguishing between people who have blue eyes and those who have brown. Why does it matter?

I would argue that our differences benefit us. They require us to look beyond stereotypes. Our differences are like having multiple passports. We can go into a selection of countries and speak their language, understand their culture, and feel at home. Likewise, our differences allow us to more easily adapt to and accept differences in others and to move easily among different groups. We don't think about individuals or the world in terms of separation and artificial divisions when we experience a broad range of experiences.

A DIFFERENT CHILD

Unfortunately, because this is not yet the world we live in, children like me become aware of our differences and the ways in which we are unlike those around us. We interpret these differences as negative, and feel uncomfortable in certain situations.

I always felt different in school, even before I understood exactly what it was that made me different. I had a lot of friends, and I was very social. The problem wasn't that I wasn't accepted; it was that I wasn't understood. People were always asking what I was, as if I had to be one thing. Are you Jewish? Or are you Muslim? If you're French, why aren't you Catholic?

Other children, and even parents, would ask me questions that I didn't understand. Sometimes these questions were rooted in racism but, in other cases, they were born of curiosity—even if this curiosity did, at times, lead to hurtful comments.

While this feeling of being on the spot was difficult, it also armed me with skills and gifts I may very well not have otherwise acquired. From a young age, I felt I could see things other people couldn't see and, therefore, knew things they didn't know. Because of the distance I felt from those who didn't understand me, it was almost as if I was able to observe situations in a way that was unique and deeper than most. Perhaps most importantly, I was able to dream uninterrupted.

This isn't to say I loved standing out, because I didn't. Things weren't as simple for me as they appeared to be for other children. As a child, this didn't seem fair. I asked my parents why they didn't give me a name that made it easier for me to blend in with everyone else. I couldn't help but think my life would have been easier if I were named Francois. Had that been my name, I was convinced people wouldn't ask me questions. I was tired of constantly explaining and justifying myself, and of answering the question, "Where do you come from?" when, in fact, I came from the exact same place as everyone else I knew.

FORCED TO ACCEPT ME FOR ME

I realized early on that I would never be like everyone else around me, whether I was surrounded by French, Jewish, or Muslim people. I would never truly be seen as part of any group. This meant I had a choice: I could either live a life of suffering, focusing on the fact that no one truly accepted me, or I could accept myself. I began to understand that more important than being considered the same as others was dedicating my life to things that were aligned with who I was.

The truth is, in some ways I was lucky. I think so many of us feel separate from those around us. We feel we're being judged, whether that's actually the case or not. My situation was so blatant that I was forced to contend with it, which turned out to be a blessing of sorts. This required me to understand that I needed to be who I was, no matter what other people thought of me.

My situation also taught me to do what I loved. One of my gifts is creativity, which drew people to me. When it came to creative endeavors, I was judged on my creations rather than myself. This made creative expression safe, and I threw myself into it. I have my mother to thank for putting me in a position to take music and art classes, as well as to play sports. Whenever I did any of these things, who my parents were and what my religion was didn't matter anymore. I was just me, expressing myself.

UNCOVERING GENIUS

More difficult were academics, which I struggled with until my early teens.

My teachers often told my mother, "Your son is always thinking about other things rather than learning. He doesn't seem happy. You should consider sending him to a technical school."

My teachers were saying that, as far as they were concerned, I was on track for a life of manual labor and applied tasks, such as working on cars and other machines. While there's nothing wrong with this sort of work, my mom knew it wasn't the life I was built for. My mom knew I was more creative, even if my teachers didn't.

"No," my mother replied every time she heard a comment like this from one of my teachers, "he will do better in school. This is just a phase."

In fact, my mom figured out my abilities long before even I did. Anytime I did something outstanding, rather than responding with praise or congratulations, she would slap me across the face and exclaim, "See? I knew it!"

When I was around fifteen, my mom was proven right once and for all. France instated its first-ever IQ test. Unlike the other tests that I didn't do particularly well at, IQ tests didn't require me to study. Instead, they tested logic and the ability to conceptualize. The test proved what my mom had been saying all along—my scores were the second-highest in the entire school.

Now armed with the information she needed, my mother made it her mission to get me into an environment where my potential was better understood. My new school environment suited me and, with these more optimal conditions, I was able to thrive. Here, I was surrounded by people who were respectful and less judgmental. The teachers, students, and parents alike recognized and embraced the good in people, and we kids were made to feel supported and as if we were capable of achieving our desires. Good conditions are so important for all of us if we are to access our full potential. Yes, we can still thrive in less-than-ideal conditions, but it is so much more difficult.

In the two years between when I entered this school at sixteen and when I graduated, I was able to make up for years of bad academics and get into the university of my choice, La Sorbonne University. I still struggled to earn my bachelor's in applied mathematics and economics, but with hard work, faith in myself, and immersion in yet another supportive environment, I was able to pull it off.

Being in a supportive environment changed my own thinking and how I operated, as well. Up until that point, I had always assumed I was stupid. I lacked confidence. All of that changed once I felt supported. I finally felt like I was part of something, rather than feeling isolated in my own world. I believed I could achieve things; in fact, I believed I could do anything I wanted to! I began to understand that all I needed to create a life I loved was to embrace what came my way, to take action, and to have a vision.

I now understand that I was never stupid. Unfortunately, in so many institutions, teaching is about uniformity. Because I didn't fit in to that uniform mold at my first school, I was deemed unintelligent. I am far from the only person who has ever experienced this; I'm just lucky that I was given the opportunity and the freedom to discover my own genius. Again, we all have genius inside of us; it's just a matter of being put in the proper conditions to unearth our own personal brand of brilliance.

THE AMERICAN DREAM

Looking back, I can see that during the most difficult times of my childhood, when I felt the most stupid and out-of-step with everyone around me, dreams acted as my oxygen. I never stop dreaming or, for that matter, dreaming big.

As a child, I dreamed of living in the United States, where I believed anything was possible. I always envisioned the US as a place that would accept and embrace me for who I was. I was itching to get to New York City as quickly as I possibly could following graduation from university. I somehow knew it was the place I needed to be if I were to reach my full potential. Somewhat paradoxically, I also assumed that in America, I would *finally* be viewed as French (and, indeed, I was correct).

I think those who are lucky enough to be born in America may not understand that it is more than just a country; it's a way of being that vibrates far beyond its borders. The American Dream lives far outside the confines of the US. I felt it all the way in France, where I knew only in America would the way I worked, felt, and behaved be understood.

Because it's still young, America is far more flexible than most other places in the world. Where you come from, your age, and a lack of experience are not barriers because, here, you can very quickly create a new history for yourself. You can embrace any experience you want to. It's no wonder people consider the United States the place to go to become someone. America knows how to celebrate dreams—the bigger the better.

Your dreams are with you at any and every point in your life. No matter what you do or don't have or what your situation is or is not, you have your dreams. My dreams were always there with me, keeping me company even when I felt most alone.

CHAPTER THREE

THE ADVERSITY GAME

―

"When everything seems to be going against you, remember that the airplane takes off against the wind, not with it."
—HENRY FORD

If there is one person I know who thrives at what I call the game of adversity, it is my friend Olivier Levy. Olivier and I have walked down some similar life paths. Both of us were born in France, came to New York, and built a business only to scrap what we had accomplished and begin again, almost from scratch.

When I met Olivier, he was living in a tiny studio in Manhattan so that he could afford to invest more into his company. This was in stark contrast to the successful, easy, and comfortable, yet predictable life Olivier had left behind in France. Now, here he was in New York, living like a student, working from early in the morning until late at night, and spending most of his free time thinking about how to crack the code to creating a successful business-to-business startup in America.

If you don't have an entrepreneurial mind-set, it might be difficult to understand someone like Olivier. "Why?" you might ask. Why would someone give up a secure and easy path in France only to come to the US and battle all of the hardships an immigrant entrepreneur faces?

The answer is very simple: "Comfort will never make you happy."

It may be counterintuitive, but it is true. A certain level of comfort will get you to a place in life that is enjoyable and serene. But chances are that comfort won't be truly fulfilling.

Entrepreneurs and creators like Olivier love adversity for what it is: a huge obstacle that ultimately provides the satisfaction of overcoming it. The feeling is a lot like surfing a big wave. You know the wave can beat you up and take you down, but the thrill that comes from standing up on your board and riding the water makes the risk entirely worth it.

Oh! And, by the way, thanks to his resilience and passion, Olivier did ultimately establish a very profitable business in the US. He stood up and rode the wave.

A JOURNEY INTERRUPTED

As both Olivier and I can attest, it's good that the American Dream is so alluring because getting through the United States' visa process requires a lot of motivation and stamina. Talk about an obstacle! I think it's fair to say it was literally more difficult to get my temporary American work visa than it was to graduate from university, and this was pre-9/11! I think this is yet another thing most Americans are unaware of: how incredibly difficult it is for a foreigner to earn the right to spend more than three months in the US.

When at last I was awarded a visa, Noemie and I booked our plane tickets to America for September 12, 2001. On September 11, my mother called and told me something had gone horribly wrong in New York City, where I was scheduled to arrive the following day. I turned on the radio and listened in horror to the description of the Twin Towers tumbling down. Our flight for the next day—along with every other flight to America—was cancelled. Even worse than transportation issues, the job offer I had used to obtain my temporary work visa was rescinded.

Despite the tragedy, I was still insistent that I must move to America as soon as the travel ban was lifted. My mother begged me not to go, and everyone I knew told me I was crazy, but I believed now more than ever that America was my destiny. It took another ten days until I was able to leave for New York. All of my previously well-laid plans were now worthless. Noemie and I were coming to America with nothing. For all intents and purposes, we were coming on a vacation, with no job prospects in sight and $1,000 in our pocket.

THE CHOICE THAT CHANGED MY LIFE

When we finally arrived in New York, even I had to wonder if I was crazy. As our plane began its descent into LaGuardia, I could see the mushroom of smoke that still lingered over the city like a dark bubble. A week and a half after the terrorist attack, the buildings were still smoldering.

Despite the state of Manhattan when we arrived, to this day I'm convinced that my decision to continue on to New York City, despite all logic, is the choice that ultimately changed my life—even if it was crazy (which it was). But at the time, coming to Manhattan didn't feel like a choice—it felt more impossible *not* to come than it did to come, despite all of the chaos.

Upon arriving in New York, I made ends meet by doing delivery work for restaurants and cobbling together odd jobs here and there. Despite the fact that I wasn't on any specific career track, as I'd originally intended to be, I enjoyed the experience of just being where I wanted to be and living in the moment.

Looking back, I'm not sure I would have had this experience if it weren't for my childhood. Because I was used to being different, I was able to shut out the voices of all those people who were telling me I couldn't make New York work just because it wasn't a normal thing to do. Following my inner voice in the face of daunting odds also gave me the strength to listen to and trust my gut from thereon out.

I don't think that it's easy for any of us to become who we are. At some point, we will all ultimately face adversity. If we can stare that adversity directly in the eye and say, "Okay, I can do this. Let's go!" we've already climbed halfway up the mountain. Saying yes is the hardest part; everything after that is relatively easy.

Once I was in New York City, I felt like I would be okay no

matter what happened because I had made a decision that was true to myself. This belief acted as a safety net that allowed me to start taking chances. Despite the fact that the odds were stacked against me in terms of getting a job in New York—the job market was extremely tight in the wake of 9/11, and I was a foreigner to boot—I managed to land my first position without even sending out a résumé.

I had no time to waste finding a job, so instead of going through normal application channels, I started cold-calling CEOs. I directly called a woman in one of the world's top five media agencies and said, "Let me tell you the story about how I came here." I then explained the crazy ride I'd been on over the past several weeks and ended by telling her I thought I would be a great fit for her company.

"It's funny," she replied. "I just had a meeting with my team, and we decided we need to hire an intern. Come in and talk to me tomorrow."

Three days later, I had interviewed, the job was mine, and this advertising company had agreed to sponsor my work visa. As the woman who hired me explained, "If you did all of that just to be here, I'm sure you're a hard worker, so I'm going to give you a shot."

To this day, I believe I was able to pull off the near impossible because of the power of intention. I had such belief in my path that I put myself in a position to receive a yes from people. I became the experience I wanted to acquire.

RETHINKING MY PATHWAY

For the next five years, things were great. I continued to move up at the advertising company. I felt successful, and I loved New York City. I was achieving everything I had ever dreamed of.

And then, after my father's death in 2006, I began to understand that, for as much as I had always marched to the beat of my own drummer in my younger years, recently I had fallen into a pattern that was dictated by achievement rather than fulfillment. My life wasn't a full expression of who I was or who I wanted to be.

Shortly after my epiphany on the bench, I was offered a promotion. In that moment, I realized it was time to take new action. I understood that achievement was no longer going to be enough. I declined the offer, threw away my résumé, and booked an open-ended plane ticket with Noemie to travel the world. Our first stop was a visit back to the place where it all started: France.

DISCOVERING NEW COLORS

When we arrived in France, I cracked open my father's paint set. I hadn't picked up a paintbrush in years, but with these same colors my father had used to create, I began to channel my grief as well as my general confusion about life and my place in it. I rediscovered my father through the colors he had once used, almost like we were building a new relationship and connection through the paints. Friends saw a couple of paintings of mine and asked if they were my dad's because our styles were so similar. It was almost as if our spirits had merged together and we were painting as one.

There was a great irony to this. Both of my parents were extremely artistic people, and I think they would have loved nothing more than for me to become an artist. However, I wanted to become a businessman and an entrepreneur. I equated an artistic life with a life of struggle and financial hardship, and I wanted more. I began to realize that because of this fear, I had inadvertently entirely blocked myself off from creating throughout my adult life—until now. I was taking the easy path, trying to avoid obstacles and adversity.

I found myself in the midst of a creative explosion, and it made me feel incredibly alive. I painted every day, and it was if the energy of the colors was flowing through me.

As I was creating something with the paint, the paint was also creating something new out of me. This creative act nurtured me, allowing me to see into parts of my mind and spirit that were previously hidden in the shadows.

I churned out canvas after canvas over the course of the next three months and felt infused with a new sense of peace and happiness. The act of painting reminded me of what I had known when I was younger, but had forgotten it as the need to achieve set in during adulthood: I am a creator.

For years now, I realized, I had been hiding behind academic knowledge and career success, neither of which connected me with my creative spirit. Once my creativity was again unleashed, it felt so incredibly freeing and wonderful that I knew I couldn't live without it anymore. I didn't have to be a painter, but I did have to be a creator because creating was a direct pathway to joy. I now understood that I could create basically anything.

With this creative spirit still coursing through my veins, Noemie and I set off again to see more of the world. We went to China, Thailand, and Japan. We saw new things and had no commitments other than to our own happiness and whims at any given moment. Despite all of the beauty and novelty around me, I couldn't shake an underlying sense of anxiety bubbling within me. I think it came from the knowledge deep down within me that, although our trip was finite, there was no going back to the way things were before. The future was totally unknown.

Even as we moved from place to place, I continued to foster my newly rediscovered craving for creation. No matter where we were, every day I carved out time and space to read and paint. It came to feel as if these pursuits were an integral part of my treatment as I moved through this time of grieving. To this day, when I flip through the pages of one of the books I read while on this great adventure, it transports me back to that time when I felt as if life was being created anew. It reminds me of all of those feelings I felt in the wake of losing a parent.

The death of any loved one is difficult, but the loss of a parent brings with it a specific kind of grief and mourning. When we lose a parent, we also lose a certain sense of protection. I knew that in this new world without my father in it, there was no room left for any sort of compromise. Life was too short, and I was now solely responsible for me.

THE MOST IMPORTANT CREATION OF ALL

The more I thought about creation, the more I realized it is our lives that are our biggest and most important creation. This creation starts with our thoughts and beliefs, then extends out to the people who are around us and our environment. It encapsulates our jobs, interests, and everything down to the books we read.

My new understanding of creation put all of my life decisions under a different lens. I wasn't just living a life; I was creating a life. My life. And this meant that every single decision I made was the equivalent of a brushstroke. Every single decision served as a color that would ultimately contribute to the painting of my life and the lives of those I loved.

No matter what it is we are ultimately creating, all creation starts with a feeling that is very similar to freedom. Creation is present when our minds are free and there is no friction. We can create when we can express ourselves fully and freely, with no worry or limitations, but just as we are. It's a state of no resistance, where we can observe what we are and feel good about it. It's a state of self-love and a state of mind.

GOING BACK TO WHERE IT ALL STARTED

After four months of adventure, Noemie and I decided that rather than return to New York City, we would live in Paris for a couple of years. So many things had become clear on our trip, one of which was that we wanted to be closer to family. Upon hearing this, the company I had worked for in New York offered me a job in Paris. It was obvious to me that I had to say no to the offer, even if it was the easy way out—or, perhaps more accurately, because it was the easy way out. After unearthing my creative self over the course of the past several months, it didn't even feel like a decision. There was simply no going back to the way things had been before.

My time away from New York allowed me to realize that I had been living a life based on illusions—illusions about achievement and being better than others. I had somehow fallen into a mode of feeling the need to prove myself to those who didn't believe in me. I was living my life not so much to satisfy myself as to impress others. I had a new understanding that none of what I was striving for was true. Things that are true not only make us feel good, but they also make us feel at peace—I did not feel that about the life I had created for myself in New York. The time had come to start my own company and to be my own boss. I wanted to create my own lifestyle, to be free and responsible only to myself. I needed to forge my own pathway.

Just as people questioned me when I moved to New York with no job post-9/11, they also questioned me when I turned down jobs in favor of launching my own company in France. Ignoring another round of "you're crazy" commentary, I set about launching a digital agency that created websites and, later, mobile apps. Within just a couple of months, I had clients, and my business was up and running.

Even after everything I had learned in the past several months, sometimes it was still difficult to remain focused on what mattered the most. Although I had started my own agency as a means of remaining in the creative mindset, I nonetheless quickly became trapped in that same old game—I fixated on accolades and metrics, constantly trying to achieve more and to become more successful.

STILL CRAZY

After a few years running my business in France, I felt drawn back to New York. Somehow, I just knew that I wasn't done there yet. I had experienced New York as an employee, but not as a creator. Plus, my digital agency had quickly branched out into technology and software creation, fields in which France was lagging behind the United States. I wanted the rush of being where it was all happening.

Moving back to New York meant all but scrapping the work

I had put into building my business in Paris. Again, everyone told me I was crazy to give up what I had achieved. Indeed, everyone was right—moving my business to New York did basically entail scrapping my business and starting from scratch. But there was something energizing about starting all over again, about creating from the ground up. It was like I generated my own momentum. Before long, my business was up and running in New York, and the process of starting over put me more deeply in touch with my creative self.

Yet again, being "crazy" paid off. Over the years, I have learned to take comfort in being called crazy. To me, it's a clear sign that I am on the right path, even if the right path isn't the easy path. When people call us crazy, it's usually because we are operating from a place of self-trust and confidence. We have reasons for doing things that the outside world may very well not be able to identify. Often, these reasons don't entail much more than thinking, "It just feels right." It is in these moments that I believe we are truly following our unique pathway. "You're crazy" is just another way of saying, "You are aligned with yourself." I don't know about you, but I will happily be accused of this any day!

THE VALUE OF EMOTIONAL INTELLIGENCE

Our actions may sometimes look crazy from an outside

perspective simply because we are operating from a place of emotional intelligence, rather than purely rational intelligence. Information that we derive from emotional intelligence, while crystal clear to the person feeling it, can be almost impossible to explain to our family, friends, and loved ones in any sort of logical way.

Obviously, we want our decisions to be rational, but we also want to balance this with what we know to be true on an emotional level. In doing this, we are acting from a holistic point of view, wherein our mind, body, and spirit are all firing. We are taking our entire essence into account.

In this world, there are some truths that simply can't be explained rationally. Instead, we connect with these truths on an emotional level. Information flows in in such a way that is difficult, if not impossible, to explain, but that doesn't make it any less real. I believe the ability to identify, recognize, and act upon our emotional intelligence is a key to following our own unique pathway. To do this requires that we trust ourselves.

THE MOST IMPORTANT ACCOMPLISHMENT OF ALL

I'd spent nearly a decade exploring the idea of uniqueness and blazing my own pathway to varying results, but it wasn't until my twin son and daughter were born four years ago that I truly and completely grasped how incredibly important and magical each and every one of us is. It wasn't until I knew my children that I understood, on the deepest level possible, what is truly important.

With twins, there is a natural tendency to compare children. Within a couple of months of their birth, my wife and I couldn't help but notice that our son, Zacharie, wasn't maturing as quickly as our daughter, Elia. After a while, we became a bit concerned. We spoke to our pediatrician, who sent us to a specialist. The specialist performed an MRI on Zach, which revealed he had a malformation on his brain. This information was completely shocking and, for several months, we lived under the assumption that our lives would never be the same again.

In some ways, it's probably true that our lives will never be the same again, in much the same way that no parents' lives are ever the same again once their children arrive. However, at first, all we could see were the negative ways in which Zach's brain defect would affect both his own life and our life as a family. Then, all of a sudden, my perception shifted.

I had a moment during which I understood that my entire life had been leading up to this moment. After all, hadn't I always done things differently? Hadn't I always created my own way, whether by choice or out of necessity, no matter how challenging it was? I was the guy who had been obsessed with the notion of uniqueness, ever since my moment with the old man on the bench. Of course I could handle this situation. And of course my son would be okay, no matter what.

As I came to realize all of this, a peace settled over me. I reveled in the unique essence that was both of my children. There are so many things that Zach can't do, but his incredibly unique genius is that he is totally connected to his heart and emotions in ways that most people are not. People feel wonderful when they are around Zach, and it's not just the proud father in me believing this to be true. Many people have commented on Zach's unique, beautiful nature. He is like a magnet, and people love being around him; his classmates flock to him, despite the fact that his motor skills are not as developed as theirs. Zach is at peace; he almost never cries; he naturally connects with others in a way that most people simply cannot. I call him my Little Master because he has a very special energy, almost like he has access to some sort of knowledge that I do not. For whatever disabilities Zach may have, in so many other ways, he is extremely advanced.

For her part, Elia is mature beyond her years and brimming with compassion. She understands Zach has some challenges, and she always seeks to support him in whatever way she can. Elia has an inherent understanding of and connection to people that cannot be taught. Whenever someone walks into our home, she finds a way to create a link with them. It's a beautiful thing to watch.

Of all the things I have learned about being true to myself, I have learned the most from my children. They don't think about who they should be; they just act like who they are. There is no judgment. It's a beautiful thing. My children have driven home the lesson that it is in our differences that we find our greatest power.

ADVERSITY IS THE BRIDGE

There are certain rules and patterns that seem to apply when we reach various milestones in life. When that spark starts to burn within you, and you are ready to embrace your uniqueness and connect with your essence, you may, at first, experience a feeling of peace settling over you. But after that, you may find that you are faced with adversity in the process of aligning with this new version of yourself. You can think of adversity as the bridge between the old you and the new you. I have walked over this bridge many times in the course of the significant changes I've made in my life.

I believe this adversity occurs because the best master of

all is life. Through life experience, we learn, grow, and evolve. Most of the time, life is fairly neutral—only when change is afoot does it start to feel more charged. So, if we are to become more whole versions of ourselves, we need to learn how to operate in a new way. These lessons often come in the form of adversity.

You want to say good-bye to the old, less-aligned version of yourself, but that old version of you isn't so anxious to leave. In the course of this shift from old to new, adversity is often experienced. If you're like most of us, the word "adversity" probably makes you cringe a little bit. We think of adversity as a bad thing. In this case, adversity is a great thing because it means we are moving forward in a new, better direction.

Adversity comes from the word "adversary." In this particular brand of adversity that crops up as we are evolving into a truer version of ourselves, our adversary is none other than ourselves! This is an internal conflict as we transform, as we learn to do things differently in order to walk a new path.

NOTHING MORE THAN A GAME

When adversity arises along your journey, you can think of it as a game you are playing along the way to a place of greater unity with yourself. As with any other game, even though fighting adversity may be challenging and difficult at times, it's also fun. We play games because we, as human beings, enjoy situations in which we embrace a quest for victory. And just as we choose to play games, we also choose to battle adversity because we want to win. We want to experience a truer version of ourselves. There is nothing negative in any situation that leads us closer to becoming an expression of who we truly are—it's all positive.

Just as we welcome our opponents to the field in any game, we should also welcome adversity when it appears. Give adversity a friendly handshake. Become friends with the situation. This simple action will take away much of the sting and fear of adversity.

From there, we are best served by concentrating on the process of bettering ourselves and becoming stronger as we work our way to victory. Remember, since your opponent in this case is you, your ultimate goal, each step of the way, is to be a little bit better than you were before.

A MILESTONE, NOT AN OBSTACLE

We tend to associate adversity with obstacles in our lives. The sort of adversity I'm discussing here is anything but an obstacle. In fact, we should celebrate its arrival. Without adversity on our journey to ourselves, we are not doing anything different to connect with this new vision we have for ourselves.

Adversity accelerates the process of self-realization, moving us from the state we are currently in to the person we are becoming. It helps us detach from our old paradigm and learn to live within a new one.

Another way to think of this acceleration is to imagine adversity as the wind. Suppose you are a sailor, steering a boat. You can either let the boat go where the wind takes it, or you can do the work of steering the boat in the direction you want to go. The latter scenario requires you to steer against the wind. Sure, this may not always be an easy task, but it ensures you have a direction in mind and that you are doing the work to navigate where you want to go. Adversity is just like the wind—seeing adversity in our lives tells us that we have direction.

Even during those moments when the wind is gusting and it's hard to hold on, remember that every second you continue to steer the ship in the direction you want to go is a victory. It means you are advancing that much closer to the life you desire, and that you're improving and becoming more masterful along the way.

OBSTACLES AND SUFFERING ARE NOT THE SAME THING

Adversity may take on the form of an obstacle. Obstacles are neutral. They are neither good nor bad; they merely present a challenge. Nonetheless, we often confuse obstacles with suffering. Suffering is not okay, so breaking this correlation is extremely important as we blaze our pathway to a more authentic version of ourselves.

As we've discussed, one of the hallmarks of adversity is that it expands us by teaching us and helping us grow. Suffering, on the other hand, often makes us feel stuck. Nothing changes; suffering simply becomes a state of being. Adversity and obstacles serve as a means of creating momentum and moving us forward. Suffering is more often rooted in our past. It is the antithesis of forward movement. When we suffer we often think, "Well, it's always been like this, and it looks like it always will be. I guess this is just my lot in life." We plod from one moment to the next in a victimized state, letting the world happen to us as opposed to changing our circumstances by taking action that is true to who we are and what we want.

Earlier, we discussed the notion of history and the past and how often our past accompanies us into the present moment. Suffering is a great example of bringing our history with us because it tends to come from patterns that we all have. I would define patterns as the reliving of memories of the past upon which we've created our self.

To some degree, we all have patterns, but patterns that involve suffering can be dangerous. Say, for example, you grew up in a home where your parents were fighting all the time. You finally escape the unpleasantness of your childhood home only to find yourself in a work environment that's riddled with conflict and fighting. You may very well hate that you have put yourself in a situation where a pattern is being recreated, but you nonetheless find yourself stuck in a pattern of repetitive suffering. You are stuck in your past, still suffering in it, rather than creating something new. Sure, getting out there and finding a new job may be challenging, but that's just an obstacle. It is finite, it moves you forward, it gets you in a better situation, and it alleviates your suffering. Ultimately, that is what we want.

Obstacles are like a storm that we make our way through en route to our desires. There is a purpose and vision behind them. For example, let's say you're climbing a mountain. It's hard, your muscles ache, and you want to give up, but you get to the top and have a magnificent vantage point, like a bird soaring over the landscape. Your pain was impermanent, and it served a purpose; you achieved your vision. You are better for it in the long run.

Unlike suffering (which, again, tends to appear as a pattern), we generally only have to make our way through the obstacles adversity scatters along our path a single time. Because obstacles require more action and interaction, once we make our way through them, they will likely never reproduce themselves in exactly the same way because we've been taught the lesson, and we will never act in the same way again. In other words, obstacles move us to the next level. Obstacles change us, whereas suffering causes us to become stuck.

CHAPTER FOUR

GIVING YOURSELF PERMISSION

"I've had lots of worries in my life, most of which never happened."

—MARK TWAIN

There is only one person who can give you permission to walk your own pathway and to allow your truest self to shine out to the world. That person is you. No one else is stopping you. It's both that simple and that difficult.

Without making the decision to say yes to ourselves, we're stuck. This should be an easy thing to do, right? After all, who doesn't want to decide what is right for them or what road to walk? The reason giving ourselves this permission becomes so complicated for some of us is that we're not just saying yes to a single action or decision. Much more than that, we're saying, "Yes, I give myself permission to be the person I want to be. I will allow myself the opportunity to live an existence in which everything I do, say, and surround myself with represents the true essence of me and the person I want to be."

Believe it or not, saying yes to ourselves on such a grand scale is a scary endeavor for many of us. But it's *so* worth conquering the fear. It is when we say yes to ourselves that we stand to gain the most. When we give ourselves permission to live a life that is truly reflective of who we are, we are aligning ourselves with everything that is important and meaningful to us. There is no more friction, no more doubt. When we live an aligned life, we have the opportunity to manifest more joy than we ever dreamed possible. It feels like going home. Sadly, not making this choice, not giving ourselves this chance, means that many of us are living a life outside of ourselves. It is like being forever homeless.

Unfortunately, many of us have confused the act of giving ourselves the things we want with giving ourselves permission to be who we want to be. Recently, I overheard someone talking about his goals for the year. These goals consisted of things like wanting a better apartment, a higher-level job, and a new car. It made me sad because confusing true contentment, satisfaction, and fulfillment with symbols of status is a common occurrence. How much better would our lives be if, instead of building our goals around things and acquisition, we built them around our ability to find our truest self and the pathway that most reflects that? It's only through working toward a more authentic version of ourselves that we will increase our happiness in any sort of true and lasting way. And the only way to do this is by giving ourselves permission to be exactly who we are and acting upon that.

WHAT ARE WE SO AFRAID OF?

The concept of being true to ourselves isn't exactly rocket science, so why are so many of us not doing it? It boils down to one thing: fear. That single phenomenon of fear can come in many different forms. Perhaps you're scared of being judged or afraid of an unknown future; maybe you're scared to *not* do the things your parents wanted for you. It's okay to be afraid, and it's okay if that fear is irrational (as fear so often is).

It's also important to understand that sometimes our fears aren't coming from within us—they're coming from our environment and from those people, places, and experiences we identify with. Sometimes we are so enmeshed with our environment that it's difficult to even understand when fear is coming from an outside source in the first place.

START BY FINDING THE TRUTH

Oddly, there's also a fear that being ourselves somehow means we have to be perfect—or, at least, that we have to be perfect at being true to ourselves. Of course, we become afraid once this notion is planted in our head because it's impossible to be perfect at anything, let alone something as complicated as being true to ourselves.

We don't have to be perfect at anything. In fact, we don't even have to strive to be perfect at anything in this life, including doing a perfect job of walking our own path. What we *can* do to improve our happiness is to always look for the truth in any given situation. Not the objective truth, but our truth. Once we know what is true for us, we can also identify what is not true. One decision at a time, we can start acting and making decisions in a way that is authentic to who we are.

Also know that your truth doesn't have to be sweeping and dramatic. We can better our lives and our connection to ourselves even by acknowledging and acting upon those small truths in our lives. For example, I love oranges. It is a fact that I love starting my day by smelling an orange for the simple reason that it makes me happy. I've found that when I start my day out with this little burst of happiness, I tend to have an easier time following my own path for the remainder of the day. The smell of oranges connects me with myself, and by connecting with myself I feel joy. The happiness-inducing smell of oranges is not a universal or earth-shaking truth, but it is a truth that is specific to me, and I have given myself permission to acknowledge and act upon this truth. I am sure you have your own set of little truths, whether they involve fruits or not!

FINDING ACCEPTANCE

Everything we're talking about here boils down to acceptance. It is up to us to accept our own truths, big or small; it is up to us to accept our own fears and how they are going to impact our decision-making process; and it is up to us to accept ourselves.

Acceptance also means forgiving ourselves when necessary. We must forgive ourselves for not being perfect—or even great—at every single moment. Again, all we have to do is be ourselves. Once we accept and (when necessary) forgive who that is, we can begin to be a part of something bigger than ourselves.

ASSUMING RESPONSIBILITY

The word "responsibility" is derived from the Latin root *respons*. In order to respond, there must first be a question—so what is it that we are answering by choosing to be responsible? I believe we are responding to the question, "Do you want to give yourself permission to become who you are?"

To embrace responsibility to ourselves, we have to accept the fact that we are important. We have to overcome our fears, look for and be willing to accept the truth, and respect who we are, whatever that may mean. We have to respond to a life in which our actions, behaviors, and decisions all connect back to our essence. We must be true to ourselves in our actions and, whenever possible, avoid compromise. Being true to ourselves means that our whole self is involved in whatever it is we are doing at any given moment.

It's also important to understand that being responsible to ourselves doesn't always mean saying yes. Sometimes saying no to those things that don't ring true to us is just as important. Just as we need to say yes to those things that resonate with us, we also need to take the right action by saying no to those things that don't speak to who we are or who we want to be. Of course, saying no comes with its own set of problems. We have to reconcile ourselves with things like refusing those we love or giving up money in a case where there's a task or work that doesn't align with our true self.

Saying no can look different in myriad ways. For example, two years ago I realized I wasn't focusing enough, and my work was going a bit more slowly than it once had. At the time, I was having two to three glasses of wine every other day. Not a lot, but enough that I suspected saying no to alcohol would probably bring me into better alignment with who I wanted to be and what I wanted to accomplish. Sure enough, after just a few days, I experienced a massive surge of energy, my brain felt quick and nimble, and I was sleeping better. There's no doubt that saying no in this situation made me feel better and more like myself, but that still doesn't mean it's easy. I would be lying if I said going to the bar with my friends is still the same experience it once was.

While some of these concepts are simple, I don't mean to imply that they are by any means easy. They involve us bringing all of ourselves to the table and being completely at one.

Being Responsible to Our Talents

There is another specific type of responsibility I would

like to discuss, and that's our responsibility to our gifts and talents. Although it may be programmed into some of us that acknowledging our talents constitutes a certain brand of arrogance, when we look at life through the lens of being true to ourselves, it is our responsibility to bring our talents to the surface.

Despite what some may say, we are not all equally talented. We all have talents and gifts, yes, but in different capacities. Of course, we shouldn't lord our talents over others, but it is our responsibility to share them. We create harmony when we capitalize on our unique talents because this connects us with others who can use or derive pleasure from our gifts. It also helps us be more aware of the talents of others.

You are not an average person, and neither is anyone else. Average is a fake number.

CHAPTER FIVE

BECOMING A CREATOR

"A journey of a thousand miles begins with a single step."
—LAO TZU

I believe that you become a creator in that moment when you realize you always have been one. So in a way, becoming a creator is not a transformation, but an out-of-time experience. We don't have to become, we just have to be and to allow who we already are to present him- or herself to the world.

In the decade I have been working in technology, I have noticed a couple of things while creating software or mobile applications. If you look at a particular type of technology or software, there are numerous rules and constraints that you have to follow to make it work, from the language to system access to design and user experience. All of these things make the process complex, and you may think that the only way to succeed is by executing programs and complex tasks. It may seem as though there is absolutely no freedom in terms of how to do things. Where is the creativity?

I think this has a lot in common with what so many of us experience in our day-to-day lives. Most people think there are so many processes and rules to follow that there's no room to express who they are. Rather than feeling like a creative, they feel like a robot.

It is true that we have to follow social, professional, and economic rules. However, I think there can still be freedom and creativity in everything we do. The idea is not to break the rules, but to create a space in which you identify how things can be, and in which you are able to see the unlimited potential that exists even within the confines of rules. In a way, you need to be able to create free space in every condition and activate your creativity independent of your circumstances.

When I create new software, I don't look at the data most of the time, I don't look at the competition, and I don't look at the market or the money first. I don't think about how difficult it will be to create what I want to create, either. Instead of all of this, I start with a dream about the ideal product or service that I want to release. I start with my own vision, even when I am working with clients.

To help create that space to be free and visualize, I go to a quiet place like a riverside or park, where I can let inspiration flow and think creatively. If I see a solution that results in a feeling of joy and energizes me, it usually means I have something to work toward. Most of the time, I just let that vision grow without trying to analyze or judge it. Constraints and rules always come later. At first, I don't trouble myself with them. The most successful projects I have created did not come from business school practices; they came from that space of free thinking and letting things happen naturally.

Whether creating technology like me or anything else, all creators need this space and freedom. It allows beginnings to occur. Creativity sparks when the mind is at peace.

A CREATIVE IMPLOSION

Whether you've acknowledged it or not, you are already a very powerful creator. When you think, when you smile, when you love, when you breathe, when you do anything, those billions and billions of neurons in your brain we discussed earlier are working together to create. They are literally creating your life on a second-by-second basis. You coordinate all of this incredible creation without even consciously thinking about it.

As a human being, you are incredibly advanced and powerful. The creator that lives inside of you has the ability to create something infinite from nothing at all. Once we begin to acknowledge and wrap our head around this power, a transformation starts to occur. When we connect with our power to create, we feel a new connection with ourselves and the world around us. We become a conscious creator.

It is in the process of this acknowledgement of our own power that everything becomes possible. I always think of this creative unleashing as an implosion rather than an explosion, because the entire process happens internally as we move from a state of unawareness to a state of awareness. It as if we merge our own potential with infinite possibility. Even if we are creating with tools and materials, the actual creation happens inside of us. The visible mechanics of creation are simply the result of that process.

ACCESSING CREATIVITY

Creation begins with a feeling that closely resembles the feeling of freedom. Creation can exist only when there is no friction, so it comes in those moments and periods of life during which our minds feel free and untethered. It is only then that we can create in the truest sense. We can express ourselves fully and freely, with no worries and no limitations. We can create just as we are, which is probably the most profound sign of a true acknowledgement and acceptance of our unique nature.

To see a perfect example of creation without resistance, step outside and look at a tree. A tree grows, expands, and blooms without questioning the process of its own creation. A tree is at peace and oneness with what it is. It carries with it no doubt, no judgment, and no feelings about the future or the past. It is free to create itself. Of course, we are not trees, but we can still look to them for inspiration as we create, whether we are creating ourselves or creating something outside of ourselves.

When we reach this point, we are basically saying, "This is me, and it feels good." Creativity is a state of mind that encompasses self-love, unity, and peace. Creation is simply an extension and manifestation of that feeling.

ACHIEVING TRUE EXISTENCE

When we exist in our truest state, we don't need external validation about who we are or the choices we make. We don't require markers of success from job positions or any other titles in the outside world. We don't need recognition. We don't need anything that comes from outside of us. We just feel great about who we are and what we're doing for the simple reason that it is true.

For me, embracing true existence is all about letting our individual essence flow into all aspects of life. We can think of ourselves as a riverbed that holds water, with the water being our essence. When it flows throughout the riverbed, the water is truly existing, uncontrolled by anything other than itself. It flows along its own path.

Wielding control and exercising resistance run counter to our ability to create. They remove the possibility for our essence to flow where it will, by putting up dams that either act as barriers or divert us from our natural course. When we act from a place of true existence, we are powerful beyond measure because we are coming from a purely authentic place.

WHAT IS CREATION?

For most of us, the word "creation" conjures up the image

of an artist. Creation—and, by extension, creators—are so much more than that. Yes, some of us create paintings, drawings, music, or dance, but this is just a small percentage of people. Teachers, businessmen, parents, and everyone else are also creating on a regular basis—this is a part of human nature, whether an individual considers himself an artist or not. We create friendships, we create community, we create a sense of safety for others. We cannot touch these things, but that doesn't mean they're any less real or valuable. The only difference is that the creations of nonartists are less often acknowledged for what they are. But just as our gifts and talents don't need to be defined to qualify as gifts or talents, neither do our creations need to be defined.

Creation is not something that can be labeled, such as, "This is a creation and that is not a creation." Really, it can be anything, as long as it comes from a place of loving and being connected to ourselves and staying true to our path. Creation is an expression of who we are, which is why it's so important to create with our whole and complete self. Since creative expression is uniquely and intimately tied to who we are, it will look different for every single person walking this planet, in terms of both the process and the end result.

ACHIEVING SELF-LOVE

Far from being selfish, self-love is the key that unlocks the treasure chest inside which all of our greatest gifts are stashed. Until this chest is unlocked, we can't share our gifts with the world through our creativity.

Just as creativity stems from a lack of resistance, self-love is achieved when we do not resist ourselves. Instead, we must accept our truest nature. Self-love is a natural state, but our ability to experience it has been clouded by a world in which we are too often educated to criticize and judge ourselves, which robs us of our freedom to be who we are.

In many instances, self-judgment stems from a well-intended place. For example, parents want their children to avoid making the same mistakes they did. In an effort to help their children avoid pain, parents often tell them what to do based on their own past experiences. Sometimes such advice may run contrary to a child's natural instincts, which work for them, despite the fact that these instincts did not work for the child's parent. Nonetheless, certain behaviors are labeled as "bad," which can lead to self-judgment. Self-judgment runs counter to self-love.

We live in a world where we are taught to value our achievements, which, again, are not us. Our successes and failures are neutral. They are just experiences. We can love or hate our experiences, but we are not the experiences. They are not a solid foundation for self-love.

To achieve self-love, we have to become acutely aware of our belief systems, which are often inherited from our family and can be passed down from generation to generation, regardless of whether or not they serve us. These belief systems can be dangerous because they show us how to love ourselves from an external vantage point rather than an internal one. When we love or place value upon those qualities, attributes, and behaviors encouraged by belief systems, we're not loving ourselves; instead, we're loving the environment in which we exist. These are two very different things.

Uncovering self-love also requires letting go of fear. We must accept our resistance to who we actually are (which is often rooted in fear) and understand that we are individuals who are made of love. This doesn't mean we're perfect, but it does mean that each of us is who we were designed to be, imperfections and all. Even though this may not feel true because of external programming, self-acceptance and self-love are our natural state. Once we create this connection with ourselves, there is no more resistance. We are free to be and to create; we are free to bring our gifts into the world.

BE STRONG, NOT TOUGH

The stronger we become, the easier it is to love ourselves. In today's world, we are often taught to be tough—but tough is not the same as strong. A tree is strong, but it still bends in the wind. In fact, flexibility allows the tree to withstand the storm.

Creation comes from a place of softness, which we tend to think of as weakness, but softness can be strong. We can cry and love and still be strong. In fact, these expressions make us stronger because when we are connected with our emotions and the world around us in an authentic way, we are connected with ourselves. We require strength to establish a solid foundation for ourselves and for who we are in the world. We cannot build upon our essence if we are not strong in who we are. Strength is acquired from the inside because what comes from within us is true and durable; anything from the outside can be swayed by external forces. To find our strength, we must go within.

CREATION HEALS

Not only does our ability to create contribute to the world, but it also heals both ourselves and others. Through the process of achieving the self-love that is necessary to create, we attain a sense of peace that begins inside and filters outward. This peace is powerful, and has a tremendous impact on our environment and the people around us.

Peace and love heal us from judgment; they heal us from overthinking; they heal so many of the things that ail humans today. They also create true action, which, in turn, results in more self-love and more peace for all of us.

Healing can happen in any number of ways, but for me, the paintings my father created healed me in the wake of his death. He left behind an amazing, colorful artwork collection that created a connection between the two of us even after his passing, and that compelled me to get in touch with my own inner creator. The creations he left behind also taught me invaluable lessons that played a huge role in altering the trajectory of my own life.

The more time I spent with my father's artwork, the more I realized he had missed out on bringing his true talents into the world on a grander scale. Although he painted as a hobby, he spent his life working in the fishing export business. There was no doubt in my mind that he could have been an artist, if only he had embraced his unique creative talents and carved a path from there. I couldn't help but wonder if he would have lived beyond sixty had he done so. Could passion have kept him alive?

Because of my experience with the creative expressions my father left behind, I was determined not to let the same thing happen to me. Although painting is not my passion or path, working with my father's colors in the months following his death did allow me to experience the freedom, self-love, and peace that the act of creating brings with it. I felt incredibly alive. I knew that I wanted to continue feeling invigorated and that the only way to do so was to live my life in such a way that I embraced my unique gifts and passions.

From a very young age, I had always wanted to create businesses, which was ironic for a child whose parents dreamed of him becoming an artist. I always knew deep down that artistic endeavors weren't where my own creativity laid, but I didn't quite have the courage or belief in myself to follow the entrepreneurial path I wanted to, either. So I spent my early twenties working for other people. Following my father's death, I understood that ignoring my true desired path was a cop out, and I couldn't do it anymore. I had to start walking a different, less safe path that truly resonated with who I was and what I was passionate about. Painting was merely the key that unlocked the door to my creativity. Once I gave myself permission to access the creator part of myself, I felt like I could create anything.

I had tasted joy through the act of creation, and I wanted

to be guided by it from here on out. I would be lying if I said I wasn't fearful, but I allowed joy to override that fear and to drive my decisions. In my life, I've found that joy is an incredible way to combat fear. In the face of joy, fear loses its power. Joy trumps fear every time. We can think of joy as a shortcut to the type of courage that says, "Yes, I can be the creator of my life." Courage doesn't have to mean suffering. Courage can just mean saying yes.

CREATION HELPS EVERYONE

Now more than ever, creation of any variety is important because there is no longer any such thing as an isolated creator. We can all share ideas. We can resonate together. We can cooperate. The more we create, the more we inspire creation in others.

As recently as fifty years ago, you could live and die with a great idea and no one would ever know or care about it. Today, we can share our ideas almost instantaneously. We are not alone anymore. We can create a community around the world in an instant.

FOUR STEPS TO BECOMING A CREATOR

Just like everyone else, I didn't become a creator; I simply embraced what I have always been. The only thing that changed is that I unveiled my true essence, and my true essence is to create. Yours is, too.

None of this is intended to make it sound like getting in touch with our inner creator is easy. Sometimes it can be quite difficult, but it is always worth the effort. In my own life and the lives of other creators I know and have worked with, I've found there are four steps to becoming a creator.

STEP ONE: ACCEPT YOURSELF AS YOU ARE

Accepting ourselves as we are means acknowledging every emotion that we feel and everything that we intuit. To create, we must be emotional beings, which is precisely what we were designed to be. This is a key point because through society, school, and our parents, many of us have been taught to keep our emotions and intuition at bay. These qualities are dismissed as inferior to logic and rational thought.

I am not suggesting that you let emotion or intuition guide your every whim, but I am recommending that you allow yourself to experience them fully, observe them, and act upon them when they are useful.

For those of us who have been trained to ignore our emotions and intuition, the idea of getting back in touch with them may be intimidating. One of the easiest ways I've found to tune in to what I'm being told is to get very quiet, bring myself into the moment, and observe what's happening in my body. Does something feel off? Am I uncomfortable? Or do I feel totally relaxed and at ease? So often, it seems our bodies know things before our brains do.

Once you've tuned in to what you're feeling, avoid the urge to editorialize or otherwise add information to the experience. Just allow yourself to be there and feel it. Just being as we are allows us to be fully present for all experiences, to be who we are within that moment and experience, and to connect with the moment at hand. We grow to accept ourselves on a minute-by-minute basis.

STEP TWO: PLACE YOUR INTENTIONS IN AN EMPTY SPACE

When we create, we are allowing our essence to flow into an empty space without feeling the need to direct it. Most of our creations and manifestations are based on intention, or visions that exist before the actual creation does. Intention, in essence, holds space for what we are going to create. When we think of the word "vision," we often think it has to involve images, but our vision for creation can be much more esoteric than that—maybe our vision is to create happiness or love. Whatever our vision may be, it then serves as the space we allow our creation to flow into.

I know this isn't the most straightforward concept, so let me illustrate. Let's take this book, for example. For me, this book is all about creation. When I came up with the vision for my book, it didn't involve writing a best seller but, rather, creating a space where others could create. From there, I allow the details to flow from me into that space (in this case, the book you're reading right now).

STEP THREE: LISTEN

Listen to yourself and your environment. Embrace the network of ideas that flow into you once you have established that space to create, whether those ideas come from within or from external sources.

STEP FOUR: TAKE ACTION

Taking action is straightforward, but is nonetheless the most critical part of creating: turning those ideas into something. It is taking creative action and filling up that empty space you've established with a creation that comes purely from you.

IT ALL HAPPENS IN AN INSTANT

While these steps may sound arduous, the truth is that, generally speaking, we create instantaneously.

Just like that, all of us can observe a new path, change direction on a dime, and create an entirely new and more authentic life for ourselves.

The first office I had when I moved back to New York City was a noisy coworking space full of entrepreneurs wanting to change the world. The amount of energy coming from this space was in direct proportion to the noise that ricocheted throughout these walls. While there, I encountered an interesting character named David Ams, who ultimately became a close friend of mine. In stark contrast to the buzz of our coworking space, David was always calm and in his own world.

David had created a service that allowed companies to live chat with their customers via websites. The service was quickly bought out by a corporation, and David realized he had to move to a new project. For a while after selling his company, that project was, simply, reading. There were piles of books spread out over David's desk, and, for almost a year, he devoured them one by one. There were books from every category—philosophy, spirituality, economics, business, personal growth. You name it, David read it. He told me he was reading in order to figure out what he really wanted to achieve.

After almost a year of this, David seemingly instantaneously created two business ideas that have not only come to fruition, but are probably two of the fastest-growing businesses I've ever witnessed. My point here is that although the spark of creativity occurs in an instant, we have to create space and nurture our creativity in order to achieve that moment. David wasn't reading to find a business that worked; he was reading to find the creator within himself.

CHAPTER SIX

THE BIGGER PICTURE

"If you wish to be loved, love."
—LUCIUS ANNAEUS SENECA

I was fifteen years old the first time I realized that I belonged to something bigger than myself. I was on a volleyball team with five other guys, and we were competing for selection in a junior national championship. On the morning of an important competition, we rode the subway as a team on our way to the gym. None of us could think of anything besides our game. We were so nervous, we couldn't even eat anything (which is really saying something for a group of teenage boys!).

In the end, we didn't make it to the final. But as I get older,

I realize the real prize of that time was the feeling of solidarity and shared excitement I had with my teammates. As is often the case with sports, this team of mine created a collective momentum. The team didn't have a hero; rather, we worked together, anticipating one another's moves, and helping usher the entire team forward however we could. We acted as one.

Twenty years later, I still value this team of mine. Not a year goes by in which we don't spend at least a vacation together with our families. Together, we have created a collective, bigger than any one of us as individuals.

SOMETHING BIGGER

In so many ways, my experience with volleyball parallels life. Once we have found and discovered our individual selves and the gifts that come with that, it's time to become part of collective action bigger than ourselves.

Up to this point, we've primarily looked at why it's so important to embrace our essence and bring it into the world in terms of our own personal happiness and fulfillment. Now, we're going to turn an eye toward why doing so is important on a universal level.

Once we unveil and begin to celebrate our essence by

walking our unique path, we naturally become a part of something bigger. Because we are more connected with ourselves, we are also more ripe for connection with the world around us. Connection starts to feel like second nature. We have an innate understanding of the place we occupy in one-on-one relationships, in groups, and in society in general. Once we understand our place in the greater world, we begin to create harmony with others. We are able to nurture our creative spirit, so we become a part of the creation of the world itself. Not only do we create our own lives, but we play an important role in creating the world around us.

Understanding that we are part of something bigger than ourselves is freeing. It compels us to spread our wings and to live and create in a bigger space. When our view of the world is limited to just our own selves, we think of our lives as sort of a cage. We are just little people, with our little slice of power, in our little corner of the world. When we see the world for the vast collective it is, we can see ourselves in a bigger context. We become more powerful, more creative, and allow ourselves to live in this bigger space. We have a new, bigger perspective. We give up our need for security and control, which is hugely freeing in and of itself.

EVERY SINGLE PERSON PLAYS A ROLE

As our understanding of the world around us and our place in it shifts into clearer focus, we begin to understand that not only does literally every single person play a role in creating the collective, but they play an important role in the collective (emphasis on the word "play").

When we reach this point of collectivity, the notion of "play" becomes extremely pertinent. No longer do we feel the need to take ourselves so seriously. We create more and more, but we also bring a new sense of playfulness to it. Life becomes more fun.

The word "play" doesn't insinuate that we start to lead lives without substance. Remember, children learn primarily by playing. As adults, we tend to forget about the importance of play, which is unfortunate because playing together is extremely beneficial for all of us. The more playfulness we bring to life and our interactions with one another, the more harmoniously we live and cocreate, and the more abundant peace becomes because we are in conflict neither with ourselves nor the world around us. We are able to accept and allow not only ourselves but others to be. Inner peace is contagious—when we feel it, we also exude it to the world.

We are like an orchestra, each of us playing our own

instrument, creating our own sounds, and bringing them together to create a gorgeous harmony. This harmony is far more beautiful than any of our individual sounds ever could ever be. Just as importantly, when we live this way, we breed happiness, and there are few greater rewards in life than that.

EMBRACING OTHERS AS WE EMBRACE OURSELVES

Understanding the universe begins with understanding ourselves. This is why we have to nurture our own essence before we begin to think about how we fit into the bigger picture. Once we truly grasp how sacred our own unique essence is, we can also understand how sacred the unique essence of another person is. We can nurture and support others, just as we have learned to do so for ourselves. In a way, the deeper we dive into our own individual life path, the more connected we can become with the lives of others.

In unearthing our own essence, we become an ambassador of humankind.

EVERY DAY, YOU HELP CREATE HISTORY

Yes, you may have your own path to walk, but your path intersects in important ways with the paths of others.

You are a creator, and you create your life. But you must also understand that your life does not exist in isolation.

Your life and the history you are helping to formulate right this very moment begins with the self and flows outward from there. The ideas that originate in your brain impact others and the world in general, both through the creations that spring forth from those ideas and from how your ideas spark even more ideas from those who you and your creations interact and intersect with. Ideas are connectors that tie us not only to those in our environment, but also to future generations. They are also the essence of creation. If you think about it, everything we are surrounded by was, at one point, just an idea.

Much like love, our ideas and what we can create from them are limited only by our inability to connect with others. The more we connect, the more our ideas can spread and grow. Just as love creates life itself, our ideas allow us to bring anything we can conjure up into the world.

Even after you are gone, you will always be connected to all of humankind through history. Your ideas and everything you create leave behind a certain resonance with those who follow you, both in your lifetime and after.

WE'RE ALL IN IT TOGETHER

When we act in tandem with the collective, we receive just as much as we give, and we are served just as much as we serve. Every single person is happier and more prosperous. We act as mirrors for one another.

Together, we can create a perfect geometry by connecting, being connected, and completing one another. To do this, we must discard our notions of "better than" and "less than." Rather than allowing fear to lead the way by focusing us on the differences that divide us, we must look at how we complete a full picture when we come together. Looking at the world through the lens of labels and differences keeps us from living in unified harmony. It allows us to keep other people out, rather than letting them in and creating a connection. Connection is so important because it allows us to create something much bigger than we could ever create on our own. There is no difference; we are all part of the same thing.

Labels allow us to stay in our isolated comfort zones. We create images of others and place meaning upon them based on where each person works, went to school, or was born. We look for definitions in these labels that don't really exist. Once we have applied labels, we can no longer see others for who they are. Instead, they merely represent something that may or may not have anything to do with their essence.

When we label other people, we also suppose that they are the same person from one moment to the next. While it's true that we each have our own unique essence, it is always transforming and morphing based on our collection of experiences, thoughts, and relationships. As the saying goes, "You never see the same river twice." Although the riverbed may stay the same, the water within it is constantly in motion. The same is true for people. We are never static because we're always getting new ideas. We are always living in flow.

Labels are also pointless because, at the end of the day, we all want the same things; we want to be happy, to have a good life, and to feel loved. We may all go about creating these things for ourselves in different ways, but our goal is ultimately the same. While our journeys may look different, we all want to reach that same destination.

If we were to look at humankind's collective journey toward achieving these aims, it might look like a chaotic collection of various winding paths. We might get distracted on our own individual journeys and our real purpose in life. When we feel unified and connected, we can help remind one another of our ultimate goals and purpose. The connections we create with others can help all of us to reach both our individual and our collective final destination.

FEELING CONNECTED

One of the primary ways we connect as humans is through that intangible and elusive quality I'll call our "spirit." We are more than just a body, as evidenced by the fact that we are conscious of our own existence.

Even if we don't have a name for the experience, most of us have probably experienced the sensation of our spirit connecting with others. It's a phenomenon that is difficult to explain, but we've had the experience of being "on the same page" or "in the moment" with another person. In extreme cases, it can even feel like a fusion. In these instances, we expand beyond ourselves and become unified as part of something bigger.

This merging can also happen on a larger level, when we feel connected to a group. Experiences like this can happen at celebrations or when we're on a team, for example. We are all individuals, but there is something more, something bigger than us when we come together in a united effort. I'm sure we've all felt this sense of connection before, even if we can't quite explain it. Our energy becomes collective as it rises and falls. We all come together for a mutual purpose, creating a collective momentum. We may even begin to act automatically, without thinking. We are connected.

In an ideal world, we will feel connected with other individuals and with society at large, not only on a situational basis, but on a regular basis. We will live and breathe as a collective, unified force, wherein each individual is extremely important to creating that greater whole.

CONNECTING THROUGH LANGUAGE

On a less esoteric level, we also connect through language, which is an extremely powerful tool. Language is energy. Every single word we use has an energy behind it, and every single sentence we put together has massive power behind it—way more power than we give ourselves credit for.

It is extremely important that we are aware of the power of language and that we use it properly. Not only does it connect us to others, but it is also one of the primary ways in which we share ideas and generate creation. It lays the foundation for so many things and is one of the main modes through which we are able to shrug off our feelings of isolation.

IN HELPING OTHERS, WE CREATE

We have discussed creation, but we have not discussed the specific brand of creation that comes from helping others. When we create in this way, we expand everything around us, including the consciousness of everyone involved in and impacted by that act of helpfulness. We can create entire movements as others learn and act accordingly based on our actions.

When we create, we are inspiring others to do the same. This might look any number of ways, but here is an example: Through a sympathetic ear, empathy, and advice, a therapist is creating more space for her clients. Movement is being created where there was once stuck or static energy. This helps the patient look at the world in a new way or from a different angle. This new vantage point may allow the patient to create something new, whether it's a new way of seeing things or a new life path. His worldview is expanded. The patient then brings this new energy out into the world and shares it with others he connects with, and so on and so forth.

When we help others, we are validating them and creating resonance and truth. We are impacting lives, creating, and allowing others to create in ways that are likely incomprehensible from our limited scope of the world. A single action applied to the well-being of even one other person can easily become much bigger, extending out into the world in ways we can't even imagine.

THE COURAGE OF THE COLLECTIVE

When we are working with the collective, we are working with far greater purpose than we ever could in our own lives because there is a greater momentum to our action. There is a bigger payoff. However, it also takes courage to work in connection with others.

Working with others requires us to release some habits and expectations. We must, to an extent, give up control when we are part of something bigger than ourselves. Although there is great strength to be gained when working with the collective, we may also feel a loss of power in the short-term. Of course, this perceived loss is only an illusion because we are always more powerful united than we are as individuals. When we become united with others, we become a wave in an entire ocean. What could be more powerful than the ocean?

CHAPTER SEVEN

LOVE ALWAYS WINS

> *"Love in its essence is spiritual fire."*
> —LUCIUS ANNAEUS SENECA

A few years after beginning my entrepreneurial career in Paris, I was given an award recognizing my work. It should have been a milestone moment in my life. Instead, I had never felt more alone or felt a greater lack of meaning than I did the night of that award ceremony. In fact, I was downright miserable. I had become so wrapped up in my work that I had lost sight of the creative fulfillment I'd originally derived from it. I had lost my passion and was no longer working for love of creation or love of what I was doing, but merely for success. I felt disconnected not only from my work, but also from friends and loved ones. I felt insecure and vulnerable as a result. Ironically, my quest for success was leading me toward suffering.

I realized that, once again, I had been distracted from my own path by the standards of success that society projects onto the world. I was successful only materially. I knew that I had to shift my focus once again, to remind myself of what success looked like for me personally and, from there, to recalibrate my path in a way that directed me back toward love, connection, and creativity. What I realized as I experienced the shallowness of receiving that award is that I would never feel truly accomplished simply by being successful in a traditional way. How could I, when it left me feeling disconnected and driven by the wrong motivations?

It was in the midst of all this that I truly understood what success meant for me: a connection with my friends and my family. That's what was real, that's what mattered. The rest was just empty. Rather than building something that could be recognized as successful from the outside, I knew that I needed to nurture those things that made me feel accomplished and successful. I needed to foster love.

The very night of that award ceremony, as the emptiness of what I had created hit me, my wife and I decided to pack our bags and head back to New York.

Perhaps you're wondering how I got off track again after discovering my creativity in the wake of my father's death. That urge to bring my gifts into the world that I had unearthed in the time following his death was only the first part of the equation. Yes, I was moving closer to myself and my path by allowing myself to create. However, what I came to understand the night of that awards ceremony is that creating for yourself alone will never lead to true fulfillment or happiness.

Creating without connection is like playing an instrument by yourself. Sure, it's compelling and makes you feel good for a while, but at some point, you start to understand that your music will sound better and fuller if you're collaborating with other musicians. This is where connection comes from, and connection is rooted in love—love for one another and love of what we are creating with and for others.

Part of what I had not learned yet when I met that stranger on the bench was how to be vulnerable. I had not yet learned that I, like everyone else, could not do everything on my own. I needed connection. It's like the saying, "You go faster when you go alone but further when you're with others." I was looking to go the distance. And to do that, I needed to reprioritize relationships and connection as the most important things in my life.

Since coming to this understanding, I now view all of the people in my life—even those with whom I may not technically have the best relationships—with profound gratitude. Each of them has sparked more in me by the connection we've shared, and I believe they can probably say the same about me.

GETTING FURTHER DOWN THE PATH

Once we arrived in New York again, I teamed up with a friend of mine to create a series of events where people could talk about the things they were passionate about, the things that were important to them. The idea wasn't to allow people to brag about their successes but, rather, to share and create connections. Sometimes those connections were formed by a speaker sharing a life regret; other times it was by sharing a secret or a talent. The most important thing was bringing people together.

The one thing we encouraged all of our speakers to do was be vulnerable. It was incredible to witness these wonderfully accomplished entrepreneurs and achievers lay themselves completely bare on the stage. This sort of openness fosters truly meaningful ties between individuals. In vulnerability, we are able to find common ground. Being a part of this forum solidified my recent epiphany about relationships and got me back on the right path—

creating from a true place and, with that, holding my connection with others to be of the utmost importance and encouraging love.

WHAT'S LOVE GOT TO DO WITH IT?

Although love means something different to each one of us, it is the driving force behind our connection with the world. Just as we want to shower our loved ones with thoughtful gifts and support, so do we want to contribute these things to our community and environment when we look at them through loving eyes.

Love also deepens our connection with ourselves. When people are looking for love in any form, they're actually looking for connection. Love is just a means to access the particular brand of fulfillment that comes from connecting to ourselves, others, and the world around us.

In today's world, we usually equate love with romantic notions of desire. However, in the greater sense, desire and love are not the same at all. In fact, desire is one of the consequences of a lack of love. There is a far greater correlation between love and qualities like generosity, compassion, and tolerance.

Although we all have different thoughts on this based

on our experiences and beliefs, I also feel that love is deeply connected to our source, or whatever it is that you personally call that thing that is inclusive and bigger than ourselves. Love is a life force. It is vitality and energy. Love connects us to the world around us. It doesn't have to be cultivated; it just is.

WE ARE LOVE

When we connect with love, we're really connecting with our truest selves. There is the physical part of our being, yes, but there is also that intangible part of each of us—call it our essence, our soul, our inner flame—whatever resonates with you. That part which animates us is a blend of love, energy, and vitality. It is within this part of ourselves that we feel that sensation of lightness and energy surge when we experience connection. You know, that unique and euphoric feeling of falling in love with another person.

Although the more universal type of love we're discussing in this book may not always feel quite like falling in love with an individual, we nonetheless experience a rush when we have a loving connection with the world. It makes our energy flow in a different, more purposeful way. The sensation of love with all is almost like a superpower.

THE TRANSFORMATIVE POWER OF LOVE

Love has the ability to transform us and to allow us to transform others in an almost alchemical way. You've probably experienced this in your own life, whether that love came from a parent, a friend, a significant other, or a more collective group source. If you have, you know that love has the ability to shape reality. It makes everything possible.

At the time when I was in the midst of those tough elementary school years I discussed earlier, schools didn't have the language, resources, or knowledge they have today. There was no common acceptance of things like learning disabilities or talents in specific areas outside of the predetermined categories of reading, writing, and arithmetic. If you were in any way and for any reason outside the mold of what was considered normal, it was extremely difficult to find a source of support, understanding, or empathy. As one of those kids who always fell into his own category, my source was my mom.

When other people said I couldn't do something, love showed my mom that I could. What she saw in me, I was ultimately able to see in myself. In seeing my potential, it's almost as though she helped create it through love.

No matter what outside sources told her about what I

could or could not do or how I should or should not be, my mom's love acted as Teflon. Her love protected who I was and my vision for myself. Even when teachers told me I wasn't smart and that I wouldn't succeed in traditional ways, my mom knew that I was and I would. In fact, as she told me time and time again, she believed I could do whatever I wanted with my life. The fact that my grades were the lowest in my class during my formative years had absolutely no bearing on what love allowed my mom to see and know about me.

In many ways, love created my life. My mother's love was able to fuel my trust in myself and in others, my confidence, and my ability to see how things connect together. To this day, there has been no stronger force in my life than her love.

LOVE AND EGO

Ego is often referred to in a negative context, but I believe it can be an extremely good thing, particularly when it is fed with love, as my mother did for me and as I try to do for my children and loved ones. I would argue it's great to have an ego, as long as we're using it to find direction and design our lives in a way that is meaningful.

When ego is built from a place of love and connection, it

can serve as an energy source, a motor of sorts, to propel us forward. When I was a child, it was almost as if my ego knew what I could accomplish, even when outside sources told me to give up. My ego could see something in me that other parts of me couldn't see. I'm sure this is because that ego of mine connected with my mom's love and belief in my potential.

Of course, ego will lead us astray when it goes overboard. But it can be a great, driving force when it is fed by love.

LOVE DRIVES US

In addition to empowering us to be who we are as people, love also energizes and motivates us. Just as love can flow back and forth between people, it can also flow back and forth between us and our passions. Love motivates and propels us forward when it comes to pursing these activities, allowing us to put them out in the world. Love provides us with a super source of energy that never gets depleted.

I have seen this variety of love at work in my own life, and I'm willing to bet you've seen it in yours as well. Love allows me to learn to do things that would not be possible in its absence, whether because of a lack of innate talent, resources, or any other number of relevant factors.

For example, I have taught myself music pieces that are so complicated that they exceed my actual ability. But because a love of music fuels me and makes me feel so incredibly wonderful and satisfied in those moments when I'm playing, I am able to exceed my skill level. It makes me unstoppable.

LOVE IS OUR LEGACY

There are so many different ways and people to love, but being a parent is one of the greatest ways to pass love along. It is through my children, more than anyone else, that I have come to understand the true power of love and connection.

As the father of a child with a brain malfunction, I have found myself in some challenging situations I never could have anticipated. When I first found out that Zacharie might never be able to walk, I woke up every morning with the sensation that rocks were on top of me, pressing me down. I felt as if none of our lives would ever be happy again. I stopped working, stayed home, and spent most of my days playing music, trying to find some solace in that.

One day, I played my guitar as Zacharie laid nearby in his crib. I will never forget the way he looked at me as he listened to the music—with so much depth and understanding. In that moment, I felt a deep, almost perfect connection between us. For two hours, I continued to play, and he continued to watch intently. It was as if the music was tying our souls together, as if we were communicating through it in the purest way possible. In those hours, it somehow felt as if I understood everything about my son and he understood everything about me. There was nothing but joy and energy and love between us. As that love washed through me, I knew that, no matter what the odds were, my son could and would achieve whatever he wanted out of life. I also knew that, just as my mother's love had supported and propelled me, my love for my son would do the same. My love was so strong that it was like an energy force of its own.

Just as joyous as the sensation of my own love for my son is witnessing my daughter's love for him. Their connection is so deep that it doesn't even require words. My daughter acts as Zacharie's bridge to the world.

"Oh, he's cold," she'll tell us, or, "He wants a drink."

It is humbling to witness.

It is also thanks to my son that my vision of the world and of connection in general were forever changed. When his first day of school rolled around, I found myself feeling unsure—not so much for Zacharie but for myself. I did not know what to expect at the special needs school he was attending. And indeed, when my wife and I arrived with Zacharie on that first day, it was clear that we were entering a new reality.

I'm sure we were not the first parents to be terrified upon entering this school, and I'm sure the powers that be at the school were very well aware of that. I assume this is why, as we walked the pathway to my son's classroom, the staff and other parents lined up on either side, singing to welcome us. It was one of the great moments of my life, watching these strangers come together and extend their own love and energy to make us feel comfortable. Seeing all of that passion, dedication, energy, and love filtered into these wonderful children and their scared parents was a gift.

I could see in Zacharie's eyes that he was amazed by the spectacle too, particularly because he's so connected to music. Together, we were part of this community, part of this school, part of this journey. We were connected, all of us, by love. And to this day, whenever I walk through the now-familiar halls of my son's school, I still feel that same connection, warmth, and support.

When we are open to and connected through the reality of love, anything is possible—for all of us.

CHAPTER EIGHT

THE END OF COMPETITION

"A man who is not afraid is not aggressive."
—JIDDU KRISHNAMURTI

I never thought I'd have a partner in business until I met Antoine through a mutual friend.

I was happy to learn that someone crazier than me existed. Antoine had big ideas and huge visions. While everyone else in the tech field was trying to cater their ideas to founders and investors, Antoine knew no limits. When I met Antoine, he was preparing a piano concert with an opera singer and, in his spare time, programming and creating a world network of nonprofits. As I observed

Antoine, I realized he worked the same way I did: creativity first, problems and market constraints second.

After working on a couple of projects together, Antoine and I decided to join forces and create Cercle, a company that helps entrepreneurs develop their ideas and businesses. Through Cercle, Antoine and I have helped give life to software and a number of successful applications. We've also helped companies identify their market, based on their uniqueness. Not only that, but together, Antoine and I are also working on a number of pro bono services allying technology, art, and music.

One of the key components of our collective work is that Antoine and I never worry about competition. We create what we love with passion. Because of this, what we do usually feels less like work and more like the specific type of joy that comes from playing and creating. Over the years, we've found that our users, clients, and cocreators are drawn to this energy.

When you let this type of energy flow for you and through you, it can flow for others, too.

THIS COMPETITIVE WORLD WE LIVE IN

For all of this talk about love and connection and the big

picture, the truth of the matter is that in the world today, most of us are trained to be competitors. It probably goes without saying that competition runs counter to so many of the topics we've discussed so far. So, in a world that is largely competition-based, how do we start to shift to a new paradigm where competition is neither the goal nor the motivation?

I'm not going to pretend that this is an easy endeavor. But I do firmly believe that the truest revolutionary act of our modern times would be extracting ourselves en masse from the cycle of competition. Of course, there will always be elements of competition with markets; that's just the reality of the structure of today's economy. But this doesn't mean that we, as individuals, have to be in competition with one another.

WHAT HAPPENS WHEN WE COMPETE

When we compete, we feel the need to be better than someone else. To accomplish this, we have to create criteria that let us compare our worthiness against our opponent's. Obviously, this comparison agrees with the concepts we've been discussing throughout the course of this book, either in terms of embracing our own and others' unique essence, or in terms of working collectively.

When we measure ourselves against others, we inherently rob ourselves of joy. When we're in competition, we can't enjoy what we've created for the sake of it; instead, we enjoy it based on what someone else has or has not created.

Another offshoot of the criteria competition creates is that it forces us all into the same box. We cannot reach our fullest potential because we are confined and limited by what the criteria are. Even when we're creative, we can only be creative to a certain extent. For example, comparing one writer's work to another's is virtually impossible, so if we want to attempt to do this, we have to create some sort of measurable system of comparison. Perhaps we decide that the more words churned out per minute, the better the writer. Now that writers are competing with this standard as the measuring stick, they may very well sacrifice their unique voice and style in lieu of word count. As you can see, competition now trumps creation and uniqueness. We can play a similar scenario out in any variety of contexts, all of which are limiting.

Competition restricts us and our unique expressions and creations. When competition lingers over our heads, we are not contributing to the world in the most authentic way possible. Not only that, but it instills in us a fear about whether or not we're doing things right. We are cramming ourselves into a predetermined space, rather than creating a space of our own.

PRODUCTION VERSUS CREATION

At some point, I think we confused the two very disparate ideas of production and creation. When I was in school, the one thing all marketing teachers seemed to agree on is that it is critical to create a product people like. They provided us with several ways of testing for likability, including focus groups and market research. For me, this sort of mind-set is incredibly destructive to the human spirit; it programs us to create only those things that already exist. This drastically decreases our chances of generating new ideas or ways of seeing the world. We become stagnant.

We produce an object or item with a purpose that is not necessarily our own and that is designed within a specific set of parameters and for a certain purpose. The idea of both products and production conjure up certain ideas about efficiency. With products, we are forced to concentrate on competition and market—which are inherently detrimental to unique ideas and creations.

When we create, on the other hand, we are drawing something from within ourselves. We create without rules. In fact, we can even create the rules themselves! Creations can be completely unique and unquantifiable. Notions of parameters, efficiency, and comparison go out the window. Also, unlike products, creations don't necessarily need to have an apparent use or to solve a specific need. They exist simply because they have been brought into the world.

When we think in terms of products, the market is limited. Products are created with certain parameters, which means there is a limited space for their consumption. When it comes to creation, there is no market because we are creating something unique and one of a kind. A creation creates space for itself, thus obliterating the need for a predefined market.

THE ONLY PERSON YOU EVER NEED TO COMPETE WITH IS YOU

When we think of the world in terms of competition, we view others as our opponents. While we certainly never want to oppose ourselves, the only true measurement we have is the "I" of today compared to the "I" of yesterday. In other words, are you a better you today than you were yesterday? That's the only thing that really matters. Since you are wholly unique, the only person you can ever be compared to is yourself.

So, rather than thinking about being in competition, we can think about being on a quest. As with any other quest, in this scenario, we are primarily concerned with where we are headed. The closer we get to our endgame—which, in this case is ourselves—the better off we are.

Perhaps you are wondering why we are coming back to the idea of self in this part of the book where we're emphasizing the collective. When we measure ourselves only against ourselves and our own path, not only do we free ourselves, but we also release and free others to do the same by removing this notion of competition.

We also release others from being our opponents. We understand that everyone else is just like us, on their own quest, walking their own path, creating their own creations in their own beautiful, immeasurable way. Instead of seeing interactions as "you against me," we understand them as "you *and* me." All parties are free to create the best and truest version of themselves, as well as to cocreate the best and truest version of the world. This is so much bigger than anything we could even dream of creating in the spirit of competition.

THE END OF COMPETITION

Here's the other thing: if we are all creating something

unique in our own inimitable way, overlap and competition automatically disappear. This simply requires shifting our focus to living in such a way that each of us explores ourselves and finds and defines our own rules. Once we've made this shift, we move away from the energy of production, which is measurable, and toward the energy of creation, which is not.

This shift will admittedly take many of us out of our comfort zone. After all, we've been trained to compete our whole lives: in schools, in sports, and perhaps even at home. We've been conditioned in such a way that these measurements and comparisons are almost soothing—they give us parameters. It is worth breaking through our comfort zone, though. Once we understand we don't have to be compared, there is a world of new space in which to expand, create, and define our lives and everything around us for ourselves. We are free to create the best version of ourselves and to bring that person into the world.

COCREATION AS THE NEW PARADIGM

When we compete, there is the underlying idea that "I'm going to be better than you so that I can replace you." This is exclusionary. It also brings with it the fear that you might be better than me, and if so, I'll be replaced.

When we cocreate, this competition, fear, and conflict go away. Instead of subtracting from the world, we create something bigger than ourselves. When we compete, I am trying to take you out of a certain space; when we cocreate, we create a space that is bigger, better, and safer for both of us.

When we cocreate, we do not attempt to force or enforce preexisting ideas on others or on ourselves. Instead, we find and create new ideas that bring us together and work for everyone involved. In this scenario, it is all but impossible to create conflict because we are working in collaboration. Everything becomes stronger.

The world today is a war of ideas, wherein the best idea is determined by the idea that the most people subscribe to. We see this competition at work constantly on social networks and in many other facets of life. Simply put, we humans just don't cocreate very well. And that's understandable because cocreation is an advanced concept. It requires us to follow an idea or path that doesn't yet exist and to unify with others in the process.

HOW DO THESE IDEAS FIT INTO REAL LIFE?

If we shrug off the ideas of competition and production, then what does this mean for our ability to financially survive in the world? After all, creation and uniqueness are lovely, but we still live in a world that requires money.

All of the concepts we've discussed so far in the book are about true abundance. If we are to create abundance, we have to get rid of any expectations; we must create simply for the sake of creating, with zero expectations beyond that.

When we manage to achieve a flow in which we are creating outside of competition, outside of the market, and outside of the notion that we are going to sell something, our life force, heart, spirit, creativity, and inspiration are able to fuse together and work in tandem in such a way that they create an energy that is in and of itself creative—the kind of energy that creates more energy and movement, like a big bang in our lives.

Energy can be anything, including money. That's right, money is really nothing more than energy, which is extremely important to remember. We tend to attach too much worry and stress to money, which only serves to draw energy away from us rather than to us because we begin to function from a place of fear. Fear is antithetical both to authenticity and to creation.

When we are able to activate this energy, we can create

anything. We no longer have to worry about competitors because we have moved forward into a space where there are no competitors.

When applied to our internal spark, this type of energy has a way of regenerating itself and amplifying. Many creators have already experienced this at some point in their own lives: whether they're creating a business, a movie, or a community, when they tap into this energy of creativity and abundance, they find that it's as if that creation isn't even theirs any more. It takes on a life of its own. You may light that spark of creation, but after that, it's your job to release the fire to go where it will. You have to let your creation live on its own and to allow others to embrace it.

LIVING IN A WORLD OF COCREATION

Can you imagine the power of a society where there is room for everyone's creations to get out of their minds and to stoke the passions of others?

This starts by releasing competition. Doing this will allow us to listen and understand one another better, to discover new ideas, and to view the world through a different filter. We can serve others and the world by allowing our truest selves, our truest talents, and our truest potential to rise through to the surface and create, uninhibited. We can allow the whole world to benefit from our uniqueness. We can create to help the world and one another, rather than to out-produce or otherwise beat our competitors.

Competition divides and isolates us. If we can get rid of it and move toward cocreation, everything will look different. If we can see the world through that lens and, more importantly, act through that lens, everything will change. We will be emotionally and creatively fulfilled. We can experience joy of untold levels on a daily basis when our focus is not on surviving but, rather, on contributing. A cocreating society is inherently an abundant society that will shed the types of conflict and abuse we know today. If my focus is to put my true, whole self toward helping and serving you, and you and everyone else are doing the same, we can all live in abundance and power. We will no longer have to waste our energy producing things that are not aligned with our true selves. We will be more connected to ourselves than ever before by using the highest level of our potential to elevate the collective.

Why hold on to competition when the truth of the matter is that we can all win in ways we can't yet even begin to fathom?

CONCLUSION

THE PATH TO GREATNESS

"The road is life."
—JACK KEROUAC

My grandfather had lived in Tunisia for thirty years when he decided to migrate to Morocco to create an artisanal olive oil factory. Another thirty years later, he moved to Paris, the city where I was born, with his family.

My grandfather loved having family dinners at a particular Tunisian restaurant, a rarity in Paris at the time. Whenever we had these dinners, my grandfather would always bring a flask of olive oil with him. This often confused the waiter because it looked like alcohol.

My grandfather didn't speak much, but he personified the idea of loving what you do. He spent his life collecting, loving, cherishing, and eating olive oil, to the point where he couldn't enjoy a meal without a spoonful of it.

He passed away twenty years ago, and to this day, he serves as a source of inspiration to me. Sometimes I imagine him stopping his car next to a small path as the beautiful Moroccan sun sets, touching the branches of an olive tree and thinking about how good the harvest will be as nature whispers all around him.

I am now in a position to become a source of inspiration for my children. It is time to start thinking about the things I'd like to pass on to the present and future generations. Since I come from a nomadic family, I have every reason to believe the next generation will be nomads as well. Here is what I'd like to leave to these future generations, for whom immigration will probably mean going to the moon or traveling around the stars.

GREATNESS IS A PATH

Greatness is not a destination but the pathway itself. We achieve greatness when we allow ourselves to experience our voice, our life, and our self in our own way. Once we start letting these elements dictate our path, life will take on a momentum of its own. We will move from a state of being unaware or unaccepting of ourselves to letting our spark ignite and our light shine bright.

We can experience greatness on a regular basis, even when our moment-by-moment experience isn't perfect. When we know that what we are doing is good for ourselves and good for the world at large at any given moment, every moment of our lives will be great, whether it is a moment of adversity or success, abundance or sadness.

Greatness isn't about feeling good, it's about being conscious of everything in every moment. We are great when we allow ourselves to experience everything and do so from a true and authentic place. It is when we claim ourselves and our life. Whether or not we receive positive feedback from the rest of the world in the midst of this is irrelevant; in fact, when we're walking in greatness, we may often find that adversity improves us.

The mark of a great life is one in which the spark of creation burns brightly and constantly inside of us. This spark remains sheltered from external events and experiences. It is constant, regardless of everything and everyone around us.

EVERY MOMENT IS A CHANCE FOR GREATNESS

Greatness is not about attaining or becoming, and it's certainly not about being something different from what we already are. It is about true action or infusing meaning into everything we do. Every single action we take is directed by our truest self and connects us to something bigger. This is how we remain constantly tapped into our creative power.

Action with meaning has far more power than action without meaning or action out of obligation. When we take true action, we are constantly aware of why we're doing what we're doing. We're experiencing every single moment. We remain constantly tapped into ourselves.

It's important to understand that true action doesn't discount small action. Sometimes the smallest actions can be the most meaningful. These smaller actions ultimately build the biggest truth, which is you.

When our actions are true, we create more space in our lives for even more action because we create more freedom for ourselves. In addition to creating more space for ourselves, we also create more energy within that space, which attracts the right people, things, and events into our lives. Everybody and everything loves creative, positive energy. We are drawn to it. Energy created by true action compounds itself, throwing more good energy into the world for more good, more connection, and more creation. We all have this ability; all we have to do to tap into it is to discover ourselves.

THE CHOICE IS YOURS

You now have a choice to make: What are you going to do with your potential? Even the most beautiful, profound creations start with a single choice—choosing yourself. Only you can give yourself the power to create a life that feels like a constant flow of true action, like a contribution to the world, like a connection to something bigger.

I started to make that choice the day my dad died. If I could go back and talk to that younger version of myself, I would tell him that it's okay to lose what we perceive as our power. It's okay to abandon everything we know because it's only by doing this that we stand to gain far more power than we could ever fathom.

All of this is simple but not easy. We don't have to compete; we don't have to acquire new skills. We can just be ourselves. We can just let go. It's only when we allow everything else to empty out of us that we can begin to exist in a truly meaningful way.

BACK TO THE BENCH

To this day, I still think back to that old man on the bench and how profoundly he touched and forever changed my life in just a few moments' time. I felt then—and still feel all these years later—that he somehow held the essence of my father, who was always so concerned about how everyone around him was feeling.

At one point during our conversation that day, the old man leaned toward me conspiratorially. "You know," he chuckled, "I've been here every morning for twenty-five years. If I wasn't here cheering everyone up every day, this neighborhood would collapse."

In that moment, it made perfect sense to me that, without his kindness, the neighborhood actually might just collapse. But what I now understand is that it goes a bit deeper than that. Each and every one of us has a tremendous impact on those we come in contact with, whether our interactions are instantaneous or last for a lifetime. More than simply keeping each other from collapsing, we all have the incredible ability to empower and lift each other up so we can all achieve our highest and truest potential.

YOUR POWERFUL LIFE BEGINS HERE

Despite the fact that many of the ideas in this book are

esoteric, I want to be crystal clear about one thing: I am not encouraging you to be passive in your life or to wait for things to happen. To achieve all of this requires rigor. And there is so much to gain: freedom, creativity, a new space for yourself in the world, and ultimately, an entirely new paradigm.

To accomplish this, you must dig deep to discover and unveil yourself. It will take discipline because true action is something that must be enacted in every moment of our lives. It requires extreme responsibility. You will create a tremendous amount of momentum as you go, but you will need it. Following your own path won't always be comfortable. But you will experience more joy than you can even fathom by living a life that is truly yours.

ACKNOWLEDGEMENTS

The Belgian novelist Amélie Nothomb once said, "Everything we love becomes fiction." I'd like to amend this slightly to read, "Everything we love becomes our story." Thank you to all of the people who have played a key role in this beautiful story that is my life.

I would to thank Dan Bernitt for being such a great listener, dating back to when this book was nothing more than just a few pages in a notebook. Your enthusiasm and guidance have been key.

None of this story would have been told without Nikki Van Noy Faulls and Katherine Songster, who have accompanied me in this process with all their talent and wonderful attention.

I'd like to thank my mother for being my mother. I wouldn't have picked anyone else if I'd been given a choice. I'd like to thank my father for showing me the path of the free spirit with all the colors of life.

I want to thank Noemie, my wife, for sharing our life and our love and for being faithful throughout both the storms and the sunny afternoons. I am grateful to her for joining me in this constant quest to be more than our individual selves together.

To my children, who brought unconditional love and strength to our family.

To my family, my cousins, and my uncles, who are with me even when I am away.

I also would like to thank the father I never had, who will recognize himself.

I am grateful to all of you beautiful characters who played key roles in my life.

And finally, thank you, life, for all of the beauty and the unexpected situations that have made me a man.

ABOUT THE AUTHOR

SERGE KARIM GANEM is a serial entrepreneur who has won awards for his work and has been profiled in major publications in France and the United States. After founding his first company at age twenty-one, he went on to start the first cloud computing company in Europe. Now based in New York City, Serge is the cofounder of Cercles.co, a digital agency and software development company.

His foundation, Itisnow.org, is dedicated to helping children with special needs develop and grow their abilities using art and technology.

www.ingramcontent.com/pod-product-compliance
Lightning Source LLC
LaVergne TN
LVHW051522070426
835507LV00023B/3242